AMERICA'S TOP SECRET TREATY WITH ALIEN LIFE FORMS
PLUS THE HIDDEN HISTORY OF OUR TIME

Commander X
And The Committee Of 12 To Save The Earth

LET THERE BE LIGHT

AMERICA'S TOP SECRET TREATY WITH ALIEN LIFE FORMS
PLUS THE HIDDEN HISTORY OF OUR TIME
by Commander X
And The Committee Of 12 To Save The Earth
With additional material by Sean Casteel and Timothy Green Beckley
Edited by Timothy Green Beckley
This edition Copyright 2016
by
Timothy Green Beckley dba Inner Light - Global Communications

Revised Edition

Published in the United States of America By
Global Communications/Conspiracy Journal
Box 753 · New Brunswick, NJ 08903

Staff Members
Timothy G. Beckley, Publisher
Carol Ann Rodriguez, Assistant to the Publisher
Sean Casteel, General Associate Editor
Tim R. Swartz, Graphics and Editorial COnsultant
William Kern, Editorial and Art Consultant

Sign Up On The Web For Our Free Weekly Newsletter
and Mail Order Version of Conspiracy Journal and Bizarre Bazaar
www.Conspiracy Journal.com

Order Hot Line: 1-732-602-3407
PayPal: MrUFO8@hotmail.com

CONTENTS

The Truth Of The Matter—Timothy Green Beckley 1

Establishing Crucial "Facts" About The Alien Treaty—Sean Casteel 5

The Hidden Time Line 23

A Shocking Look Inside The Government-Alien Exchange Program—
Timothy Green Beckley 51

Exposed: The Ultimate Deception—Commander X 61

Crashed Saucers, Aliens In Captivity, And A Cosmic Exchange Program 67

A "Classified Top Secret—Do Not Divulge" File 79

Behind The Mask Of John Lear 81

Air Force Lieutenant's Inside Story Of The Government's Policy Of Silence ... 95

Public Lecture By Mel Noel 98

Aliens Held Prisoner By Earth Governments 116

The Invitation To Meet A "Visitor" In The Pentagon 121

What The President Knows 126

Jimmy Carter Sees A UFO 128

President Eisenhower Meets With The Aliens 130

An Astronaut Becomes Involved In A UFO Landing 132

Startling Revelations From a Man Of God 134

Ronald Reagan—Mystery Man 138

Robert Kennedy's Devotion To The Cause Of The Space Brothers 139

Suppression Of The Truth 141

Jimmy Carter's Close Encounter 143

The Case Of Raymond Manchester 147

Above A "Top Secret" Classification 153

Underground Bases 155

Those Who Chose To Tell The Truth 158

This book is dedicated to those few brave souls who have risked their very lives to leak the story of the century to a public that has long been kept in a state of "blissful ignorance."

This conspiracy leads right up to the front gate of the White House, and behind the Kremlin walls, and involves the cover-up of an "Above Top Secret" agreement forged between the military and a group of aliens referred to as the EBEs (short for Extraterrestrial Biological Entities).

As part of this conspiracy, the government has literally "sold out" our citizens by extending to the EBEs the right to abduct thousands of humans and to plant monitoring devices in their brains, in exchange for technical and scientific data.

Initially, the authorities believed these short, grey-skinned humanoids were friendly, but soon learned that their avowed purpose was genetic duplication and the ultimate domination of our globe. To this extent, they have seized several, highly classified, underground laboratories where they have proceeded to develop a form of crossbred "Super Being. "

Our only hope for survival, says Commander X, is a second group of benevolent extraterrestrials—most commonly referred to as the "Nordic-types"—who believe in the universal law of "non-interference." Those aliens have taken our side in a cosmic "spiritual war"that pits the forces of "Light and Darkness" against each other for the minds and bodies of humankind, with the Earth and our sky bemg utilized as a background for the confrontation best known as THE ULTIMATE DECEPTION.

An alien—Nazi Hybrid by Carol Ann Rodriguez

"Monka"—A Martian by Carol Ann Rodriguez

A Tall Grey by Carol Ann Rodriguez

A Venusian Lady by Carol Ann Rodriguez

Alien by Carol Ann Rodriguez

THE TRUTH OF THE MATTER
By Timothy Green Beckley

Some will say that this is among the most absurd conspiracy books ever published. It deals with a subject that has been closely guarded and – if true – one that has also been smothered beneath an avalanche of disinformation and confusion by "the powers that be."

The rumors started way back in the 1950s, when it was alleged that President Dwight Eisenhower had met with aliens some have dubbed the "Etherians" at Edwards Air Force Base (then known as Muroc). It is public knowledge that, before his exiting the Oval Office, Ike would make a series of shocking comments regarding a "military/industrial complex" he saw encroaching upon our society and our freedoms.

There are some, and I would tend to include myself in this category, who feel that Eisenhower made these statements because he saw that there was a massive cover-up and that that cover-up might have been concocted to conceal both his secret meeting with aliens and its aftermath.

Here is an abridged version of his comments:

My fellow Americans:

Three days from now, after half a century in the service of our country, I shall lay down the responsibilities of office as, in traditional and solemn ceremony, the authority of the Presidency is vested in my successor.

This evening I come to you with a message of leave-taking and farewell, and to share a few final thoughts with you, my countrymen.

Like every other citizen, I wish the new President, and all who will labor with him, Godspeed. I pray that the coming years will be blessed with peace and prosperity for all.

Our people expect their President and the Congress to find essential agree-

ment on issues of great moment, the wise resolution of which will better shape the future of the Nation.

We now stand ten years past the midpoint of a century that has witnessed four major wars among great nations. Three of these involved our own country. Despite these holocausts, America is today the strongest, the most influential and most productive nation in the world. Understandably proud of this pre-eminence, we yet realize that America's leadership and prestige depend, not merely upon our unmatched material progress, riches and military strength, but on how we use our power in the interests of world peace and human betterment.

This conjunction of an immense military establishment and a large arms industry is new in the American experience. The total influence – economic, political, even spiritual – is felt in every city, every State house, every office of the Federal government. We recognize the imperative need for this development. Yet we must not fail to comprehend its grave implications. Our toil, resources and livelihood are all involved; so is the very structure of our society.

In the councils of government, we must guard against the acquisition of unwarranted influence, whether sought or unsought, by the military/industrial complex. The potential for the disastrous rise of misplaced power exists and will persist.

We must never let the weight of this combination endanger our liberties or democratic processes. We should take nothing for granted. Only an alert and knowledgeable citizenry can compel the proper meshing of the huge industrial and military machinery of defense with our peaceful methods and goals, so that security and liberty may prosper together.

Akin to, and largely responsible for the sweeping changes in our industrial/military posture, has been the technological revolution during recent decades.

In this revolution, research has become central; it also becomes more formalized, complex, and costly. A steadily increasing share is conducted for, by, or at the direction of, the Federal government.

Today, the solitary inventor, tinkering in his shop, has been overshadowed by task forces of scientists in laboratories and testing fields. In the same fashion, the free university, historically the fountainhead of free ideas and scientific discovery, has experienced a revolution in the conduct of research. Partly because of the huge costs involved, a government contract becomes virtually a substitute for intellectual curiosity. For every old blackboard there are now hundreds of new electronic computers.

The prospect of domination of the nation's scholars by Federal employment, project allocations, and the power of money is ever present and is gravely to be regarded.

You and I – my fellow citizens – need to be strong in our faith that all nations, under God, will reach the goal of peace with justice. May we be ever unswerving in *devotion to principle, confident but humble with power, diligent in pursuit of the Nation's great goals.*

To all the peoples of the world, I once more give expression to America's prayerful and continuing aspiration:

We pray that peoples of all faiths, all races, all nations, may have their great human needs satisfied; that those now denied opportunity shall come to enjoy it to the full; that all who yearn for freedom may experience its spiritual blessings; that those who have freedom will understand, also, its heavy responsibilities; that all who are insensitive to the needs of others will learn charity; that the scourges of poverty, disease and ignorance will be made to disappear from the Earth, and that, in the goodness of time, all peoples will come to live together in a peace guaranteed by the binding force of mutual respect and love.

Certainly these remarks serve to indicate that something during his two terms in office had a tremendous effect upon a President who was a stanch conservative and a General not known for his sensitivity and enlightenment. What had impacted his conscience so much that he would publicly soften his views on a variety of topics?

Could it have been due to his rumored meeting with a group of Ultra-Terrestrials? And the subsequent fact that these assemblages were never spoken about in public, that he had been forced to keep quiet about them to the point where an absurd "cover story" was created involving a presumed visit to the dentist?

Going a step further, if Eisenhower did have a prearranged, clandestine meeting with aliens, what was the result of their conversation? What were the discussions all about? What future policies might they have outlined? And, at the end of the meeting(s), did we simply shake hands and say "see you" as we walked away?

There are some, including Commander X, the retired military intelligence operative who supplied the majority of these pages, as well as ace pilot John Lear, who say that these conferences with Eisenhower led up to an actual agreement – AN INTERPLANETARY TREATY – being "signed and sealed" by both sides.

And, if this is true, what was in this treaty?

And have both sides upheld it?

Or is some secret group laughing behind our backs, having set up the entire scenario as part of some sinister disinformation program about which we can only guess the motivations and outcome?

For those wishing to investigate the disinformation premise, we suggest you stream a video called "Mirage Men," which relates the condemnable antics of one particular military operative who admits that he hoaxed numerous scenarios in order to misdirect certain UFO researchers in their investigative work.

He is also suspected of being behind the creation of the MJ-12 documents, which he has never fully admitted. He may have at least "shaped" the documents according to some directive he was given by his superiors to provide false information to the UFO-believing community. His name is Richard Doty and he is known to have worked for the U.S. Air Force Office of Special Investigations.

But could it be that Doty was so unscrupulous that he just made the entire thing up and now, to cover his own ass, claims he was ordered to commit such dastardly deeds by his military bosses? No way of telling for sure, what with Doty's penchant for distorting the truth on the behalf of a public he seems to hold in contempt – but isn't that the way of a whole lot of policymakers today? Eisenhower was on to this fact, wasn't he, Doty, ole boy?

THE TREATY

But we are here largely to talk about a Treaty – a Treaty between the U.S. shadow government and the aliens. Is there such a highly positioned Treaty? What ground did the Treaty cover? And have both sides abided by it? Or is this only another subterfuge to pull the proverbial wool over our eyes and keep our heads stuck in the sand of ignorance and eternal bliss?

If you believe Commander X and the rantings of a rather disturbed Bill Cooper, then you will know that there is such a Treaty. You will know that the aliens did not keep their part of the deal and are abducting humans freely as well as committing other atrocious deeds that would no doubt pass muster with the Galactic Federation, if it turns out there indeed is really such a governing entity.

Do we have here a conflict between the history that we have come to accept as taught through textbooks and "CNN" and a hidden, alternative history that is being kept from us, supposedly for our "own good?" Some of the elements of this alternative history are hard to swallow and you may not necessarily buy into them as outlined in these pages. But they are certainly food for thought, something for us to ponder and come to our own conclusions about. Our readers are known as independent thinkers and philosophers who at least want the opportunity to make their own decisions in such highly contested matters.

Bless you and keep you from harm in all things.

EXPOSING CRUCIAL "FACTS" ABOUT THE ALIEN TREATY
By Sean Casteel

First, you have to accept the premise that we are not alone in the universe. Then you have to agree intelligent life has arrived here and that it consists of a group or groups of ETs who are more advanced than we are and who can travel freely through time and space. Then we must ask ourselves if we are important enough that they would endeavor to set up some sort of ongoing "relationship" with us. And why the United States? Because we are thought of as the most powerful nation on the planet? There is a growing conviction among a certain "fringe" group of Ufologists that we have gone so far as to sign a treaty with at least one group of aliens, possibly several.

So who signed this treaty? And what exactly does it consist of?

And – perhaps most important of all – has the treaty been broken because one or both sides did not keep to this agreement?

EISENHOWER ESTABLISHES FIRST CONTACT

Most stories about the alleged treaty between the U.S. government and a race of UFO occupants start with then President Dwight D. Eisenhower and his rendezvous with the alien interlopers circa 1954.

The story is told in varying versions and may already be familiar in one form or another to the seasoned UFO reader, but it is told again here to lay the foundation for the basic concept of this book. One of the most thorough treatments of the Eisenhower encounter is told by Michael E. Salla, Ph.D., in an online posting called, aptly enough, "Eisenhower's 1954 Meeting With Extraterrestrials."

The chronology begins on the night of and early morning hours of February 20-12, 1954, when Eisenhower was purportedly on vacation in Palm Springs and "went missing." The next morning, at a church service in Los Angeles, reporters were told that the president had required emergency dental treatment from a local dentist after losing a tooth cap while eating fried chicken. The dentist himself was presented at an official function that evening, seemingly to solidify an apparent cover-up and keep the press in the dark.

Did Eisenhower meet with aliens at Muroc Dry Lake in the California desert?

"That missing night and morning," Salla writes, "has subsequently fueled rumors that Eisenhower was using the alleged dentist visit as a cover story for an extraordinary event."

The event is possibly "the most significant that any American president could have conducted," Salla's paper continues. "An alleged 'first contact' meeting with extraterrestrials at Edwards Air Force Base (previously Muroc Dry Lake) and the beginning of a series of meetings with different extraterrestrial races that led to a 'treaty' that was eventually signed."

Salla then points to circumstantial evidence that the meeting truly occurred. One of the most questionable aspects of situation has to do with Eisenhower's Palm Springs winter vacation itself, slated to run from February 17-24. The vacation was announced rather suddenly and came less than a week after Eisenhower's "quail shooting" vacation in Georgia. This was most unusual.

On the night of February 20, when Eisenhower's presence could not be accounted for, the media began to wonder if he had taken ill or even died. Eisenhower's press secretary quickly convened a news conference and put out the dentist story. During those hours, Eisenhower could easily have traveled from Palm Springs to the nearby Muroc Dry Lake.

When one looks at the unscheduled nature of the president's vacation, the hours he was missing and the dentist cover story, a definite pattern emerges. Whatever was really happening behind the scenes was not something that could be shared with the public.

GERALD LIGHT PROVIDES AN EARLY PUBLIC SOURCE

Gerald Light, who was called a "gifted and highly educated writer and lecturer, skilled in both clairvoyance and the occult," sent a letter dated April 16, 1954, to Meade Layne, who at the time was the director of Borderland Sciences Research Associates.

In the letter, Light claimed that he was part of a delegation of community

leaders invited to the meeting with extraterrestrials at Muroc in order to test public reaction to the alien presence. Also asked to attend were Hearst papers reporter Franklin Allen, Edwin Nourse of the Brookings Institute (who had been Harry Truman's financial adviser), and Bishop MacIntyre of Los Angeles.

After undergoing six hours of "vetting," or extremely detailed background checks, the group was permitted to enter the "restricted section."

"I had the distinct feeling," Light writes, "that the world had come to an end with fantastic realism. For I have never seen so many human beings in a state of complete collapse and confusion, as they realized that their own world had indeed ended with such finality as to beggar description."

This is what the late Harvard psychiatrist Dr. John Mack called "ontological shock." Mack coined the phrase to describe the feeling one gets when first coming to realize the alien presence is undeniably real and that a total restructuring of one's former sense of reality is demanded. Light seems to be describing that shaken state of mind in his letter, which points to a consistency with what the UFO research of the ensuing decades would uncover.

"The reality of the 'other plane' aero-forms is now and forever removed from the realms of speculation," Light continued, "and made a rather painful part of the consciousness of every responsible scientific and political group."

Light says he was on the scene at Muroc for two days and witnessed five separate and distinct types of alien aircraft being studied and handled by Air Force officials with the permission and assistance of a group Light calls the "Etherians."

"I have no words to express my reactions," he writes. "It has finally happened. It is now a matter of history."

AMERICA'S TOP SECRET TREATY WITH ALIEN LIFE FORMS

Light mistakenly felt that Eisenhower would ignore the conflicts going on between various officials behind the scenes and present the situation to the public if the impasse continued much longer. Salla notes that no such formal announcement was made and Light's meeting was either the best-kept secret of the 20th century or the fabrication of an elderly mystic known for out-of-body experiences.

Meanwhile, Salla says there is a plausibility to the list of those Light claimed had joined him at the meeting in that they represented senior leaders of the religious, spiritual, economic and newspaper communities. All of the invitees were of advanced age and constituted a "wise man" group that would have reflected the conservative nature of American society at the time.

WILLIAM COOPER ADDS ANOTHER LAYER OF CREDENCE

In Loving Memory

Milton William Cooper
1943-2001

Truth seeker and revealer. Earth patriot.

The late William Cooper was a highly controversial whistleblower of great fame, though his statements would often be critically scrutinized and attacked. As for his personal background, he said he served on the Naval Intelligence briefing team for the Commander of the Pacific Fleet from 1970 to 1973 and therefore had access to classified documents that he had to review in order to fulfill his briefing duties.

According to Salas, Cooper describes the background and nature of the "First Contact" thusly:

"In 1953, astronomers discovered large objects in space which were mov-

AMERICA'S TOP SECRET TREATY WITH ALIEN LIFE FORMS

William Cooper would broadcast to the world every day via short wave radio.

ing toward the Earth. It was first believed that they were asteroids. Later evidence proved that the objects could only be spaceships. When the objects reached the Earth, they took up a very high orbit around the Equator. There were several huge ships, and their actual intent was unknown."

Operatives of Project Sigma, which worked to intercept radio signals, and a new project, Plato, tasked with establishing diplomatic relations with this race of space aliens, worked together to transmit radio communications to the ships using the binary computer language. The U.S. was thus able to arrange a landing that resulted in face-to-face contact with alien beings from another planet. In the meantime, a race of human-looking aliens also contacted the U.S. government.

"This alien group warned us against the aliens that were orbiting the Equator and offered to help us with our spiritual development. They demanded that we dismantle our nuclear weapons as the major condition. They refused to exchange technology citing that we were spiritually unable to handle the technology which we then possessed. They believed that we would use any new technology to destroy each other."

This race stated that:

*** We were on a path of self-destruction and we must stop killing each other.

*** We must stop polluting the Earth.

*** We must stop raping the Earth's natural resources.

*** We must learn to live in harmony.

Cooper writes that these terms were met with extreme suspicion, especially the major condition of nuclear disarmament. It was believed that meeting that condition would leave us helpless in the face of an obvious alien threat. We also had no precedent in history to help in making the decision. In any case, it was decided that nuclear disarmament was not in the best interest of the United States. The aliens' overtures were rejected.

"The significant point about Cooper's version," Salla writes, "is that the humanoid extraterrestrial race was not willing to enter into technology exchanges that might help weapons development and was instead focused on spiritual development. Significantly, the overtures of these extraterrestrials were turned down."

In retrospect, it seems we said "no" to the good guys, doesn't it?

THE 1954 AGREEMENT WITH THE ALIENS

A host of other whistleblowers, to include former CIA pilot John Lear and former Master Sergeant Robert Dean (who, like Cooper, had access to top secret documents) offer accounts of the Muroc meeting that agree on some points and disagree on others,

In any case, Eisenhower's February 1954 meeting was not successful. After the failure of that first meeting, the president subsequently met later that year with a race of large-nosed gray aliens who had been orbiting the Earth before landing at Holloman Air Force Base in New Mexico.

Did the aliens engage us early on, insisting we sign a Treaty with them? If so, have they led us down the garden path?

Eisenhower and/or members of his administration reached a basic agreement with this second alien race. They identified themselves as originating from a planet in orbit around a red star in the Constellation of Orion that we call Betelgeuse. They stated that their planet was dying and that at some unknown future time they would no longer be able to survive there.

The treaty reached with this gray race stated that the aliens would not interfere in our affairs and we would not interfere in theirs. We would keep their presence on Earth a secret. They would furnish us with advanced technology and would help us in our technological development.

They would not make a treaty with any other Earth nation.

They could abduct humans on a limited and periodic basis for the purposes of medical examination and the monitoring of our development, with the stipulation that the humans would not be harmed, would be returned to their point of abduction, and would have no memory of the event. The alien nation agreed to furnish a list of all human contacts and abductees on a regularly scheduled basis.

Further testimony comes from yet another whistleblower, Phil Schneider, a former geological engineer who was employed by corporations contracted to build underground bases. Schneider worked extensively on black projects involving extraterrestrials. He summarized what he knew about the earthling/alien compact:

"Back in 1954, under the Eisenhower administration, the federal government decided to circumvent the Constitution of the United States and form a treaty with alien entities. It was called the 1954 Greada Treaty, which basically made the agreement that the aliens involved could take a few cows and test their implanting techniques on a few human beings but that they had to give details about the people involved."

This same pattern of testimony is also repeated by Don Phillips, who served in the Air Force on various clandestine aviation projects. He claims to have seen documents detailing the facts of Eisenhower's meeting with the aliens and the fact that some kind of treaty was later signed.

Meanwhile, the late Colonel Philip Corso, a highly decorated officer who had served on Eisenhower's National Security Council and decades later authored the highly controversial book, "The Day After Roswell," characterized what had happened as a kind of "negotiated surrender" to the aliens. Corso wrote in his memoirs that "They dictated the terms because they knew what we most feared was disclosure."

THE ALIENS PROVE UNTRUSTWORTHY

The whistleblowers also talked about the immediate aftermath of the treaty.

"By 1955," Cooper writes, "it became obvious that the aliens had deceived Eisenhower and had broken the treaty. It was suspected that the aliens were not submitting a complete list of human contacts and abductees and it was further suspected that not all abductees had been returned."

Lear says similarly, "We got something less than the technology we bargained for and found the abductions exceeded by a million-fold what we had naively agreed to."

In October 1955, General Douglas Macarthur delivered a famous warning that suggested some extraterrestrial presence existed that threatened human sovereignty.

"You now face a new world," Macarthur said, "a world of change. We speak in strange terms, of harnessing the cosmic energy, of ultimate conflict between a

11

united human race and the sinister forces of some other planetary galaxy. The nations of the world will have to unite, for the next war will be an interplanetary war. The nations of the Earth must someday make a common front against attack by people from other planets."

Macarthur may well have been alluding to the same extraterrestrials who allegedly made an agreement with Eisenhower. It is a public acknowledgment, similar to Ronald Reagan's "little green man" speech before the United Nations in 1983, of an alien presence against whom the entire planet must one day do battle. If the aliens did in fact renege on major parts of the alleged treaty, Macarthur was perhaps acknowledging that we would eventually be in a state of all-out war with them as a consequence.

"The uncertainty over the motivations and behavior of the gray extraterrestrials," Salla writes, "appears to have played a large role in the government decision not to disclose the extraterrestrial presence and the treaty Eisenhower had signed with them."

Salla quotes from an "alleged official document" leaked to UFO researchers that makes it a crime under the Espionage Act to disclose classified information concerning extraterrestrials, punishable by up to ten years in prison and a $10,000 fine.

Which is sufficient to keep most former servicemen from coming forward with what they know. The most common strategies for dealing with former servicemen, corporate employees or witnesses brave or "foolish" enough to reveal classified information is to intimidate, silence, eliminate or discredit these individuals. This is accomplished by removing all public records of the whistleblowers that would establish their identity as credible sources. Such people could also be frightened into simply retracting what they said or having their testimony distorted to the point where it ceases to have the meaning the witness intended.

EISENHOWER AS THE "CONTACTEE" PRESIDENT

Returning to the subject of Eisenhower and the many alien contact stories that are told about him, we next examine the writings of Canadian researcher Grant Cameron. Cameron has specialized in the study of American presidents and their interactions with the extraterrestrial presence for many years and has cultivated a reputation for reliability and trustworthiness that has few equals in the field of Ufology.

According to Cameron, Eisenhower's attaining the rank of five-star General made him accustomed to high-level secrets. This was clearly evident in 1952, when Harry Truman gave the newly elected Eisenhower the "comprehensive National Intelligence Digest prepared by the CIA," which contained "the most important national intelligence on a worldwide basis." Eisenhower would write in his memoirs a decade later that the intelligence digest added little to his knowledge since he had already been privy to most of what it contained.

"What may go down as the most contentious part of the Eisenhower story," Cameron writes, "is that Eisenhower had many rumored encounters with UFOs and aliens. Eisenhower could thus be labeled the 'contactee president.'"

Eisenhower was said to be onboard a nuclear aircraft carrier in 1952 during a NATO exercise in which a large blue/white light appeared right off the starboard bow. It descended to within a hundred feet above the water and hovered as the ship moved past it before rising straight up into the air and departing. Eisenhower told the crewmen to "forget about it for now."

The ship in question was the U.S.S. Roosevelt. Cameron points out that just as Roswell was the first air force base to handle nuclear weapons, the U.S.S. Roosevelt was the first aircraft carrier to be armed with nuclear weapons. There has been a generally acknowledged alien "interest" in Earth's nukes from the beginning of the modern day UFO phenomenon, and one is reminded that the aliens who initially approached Eisenhower made dismantling our nuclear arsenal a fundamental condition of any agreement that might be reached.

Cameron also comments on the 1954 Muroc story. Ever the careful scholar, Cameron relates how the official records of the President's trip to Palm Springs are held at the Eisenhower library in Abilene, Kansas, and have been reviewed by various researchers. An archivist at the library says they receive so many requests on the subject that they have a person who specializes in dealing with those particular documents.

"All researchers agreed on the basic story," Cameron writes, "that being on the evening of February 20, 1954, during a weeklong trip to Palm Springs, Eisenhower disappeared from where he was staying at the Smoke Tree Ranch compound, owned by his business friend, Paul Helms. The records do not show how this disappearance became apparent to the press corps, but they did figure out the president was gone. In fact, the Associated Press had already gone on the wire with the story that the president had suffered a heart attack and was dead. Minutes later, they withdrew the story."

Press secretary James Haggerty hurried to meet with and calm down the press with the aforementioned dentist visit story. The members of the media accepted what they were told and the story disappeared completely when

Eisenhower was seen at church the next morning.

MORE INPUT ON THE MEETING

Cameron writes of even more witnesses to the Muroc meeting between Eisenhower and the aliens.

Further testimony about this Eisenhower contact story comes from the son of a former Navy Commander who claims that his father had been present at the Eisenhower event. According to Charles L. Suggs, a retired sergeant from the U.S. Marine Corps, his father stated the following:

"Accompanied President Ike along with others on February 20th. They met and spoke with two white-haired Nordics that had pale blue eyes and colorless lips. The spokesman stood a number of feet away from Ike and would not let him approach any closer.

"A second Nordic stood on the extended ramp of a bi-convex saucer that stood on tripod landing gear on the landing strip. There were B-58 Hustlers on the field even though the first one did not fly officially until 1956. These visitors said they came from another solar system. They posed detailed questions about our nuclear testing."

Then there was the testimony of UFO researcher and presidential candidate Gabriel Green, who claimed to have spoken to a military officer who witnessed the arrival of the spacecraft at the base. The officer said he was engaged in firing practice when suddenly five UFOs came flying overhead. The men were ordered to fire at the craft, which had no effect on the ships at all. They ceased firing and saw the UFOs land at one of the base's big hangars.

The late Eighth Earl of Clancarty, Brinsley Le Poer Trench, an English Lord best known as a pioneering Ancient Astronauts theorist and government disclosure advocate, also spoke to a witness claiming knowledge of the event. His information came from a U. S. Air Force test pilot who told him that "two of the craft that landed at the base were cigar-shaped and three were saucer-shaped. An immediate security blanket was thrown on all of Muroc. The craft were placed in a hangar, and men returning from leave were not allowed back on base."

Brinsley's source told him that he was one of six people at the meeting. The meeting had been requested by the aliens who "looked humanlike, but not exactly."

The aliens stated that they wanted to start an "educational program" to make the population "aware of their presence." Eisenhower answered that he did not think the population was ready, to which the aliens replied that they would continue to make isolated contacts with people. This upset Eisenhower greatly.

Cameron notes that this alleged meeting took place just one week before a major nuclear test explosion at Bikini Atoll in the Marshall Islands. The test went totally out of control, being 250 percent more powerful than expected and resulting in a bomb 1,000 times the power of the bomb dropped on Hiroshima. A total of 5,000 square miles were contaminated and two islands had to be evacuated because the residents were made sick by the radioactive fallout. Those evacuated have never returned.

"Did the aliens know this" Cameron asks, "and was the meeting a warning? We will probably never know."

THE TREATY COVER-UP FROM A BRITISH PERSPECTIVE

In a posting on the website UFO Digest, writer Ian Brockwell reported that, according to declassified files released by the U.K.'s Ministry of Defence, Winston Churchill may have ordered a UFO sighting to be made secret. He was reported as having said at the time that "This event should be immediately classified since it would create mass panic amongst the general population and destroy one's belief in the church."

The UFO – believed to be triangular in shape – was sighted over the east coast of England by an RAF reconnaissance plane returning from a mission in France or Germany towards the end of World War II. One source for this story claimed to have been present when Churchill and Eisenhower discussed how to deal with the UFO encounter. Which means Eisenhower had secret knowledge of the extraterrestrial presence going back at least as far as the war.

Another British source for inside information is James Casbolt, a former MI6 agent. In his online posting, called "Underground Bases, Missing Children and Extraterrestrials: What You Need to Know for Your Future," Casbolt confesses to having participated in covert cocaine trafficking for the British intelligence agency working in cooperation with the IRA in London. He writes that he is going public with his story in order to protect himself and his family.

"If any of us were to come to a premature end," Casbolt says, "it would only add more credibility to what I am saying. The global drugs trade run by many factions of the global intelligence community cooperating together (MI6, CIA, MOSSAD, etc.) is worth at least 500 million pounds a year. MI6 controls many of the other intelligence agencies in the world. MI6 created the CIA in 1947 and still controls them today. This 'black ops' drug money – or in classic Orwellian terms, MI6/CIA 'non-appropriated funds' – is being used to fund government and military projects classified 'Above Top Secret.' These operations include a huge worldwide UFO cover-up and the building and maintenance of deep underground military bases, or 'D.U.M.B.s'"

Casbolt reaffirms the 1954 Eisenhower/Muroc story, calling it an "unsuccessful effort to reach an agreement on the U.S.'s thermonuclear weapons program. The stumbling block to these negotiations was that these ETs were not willing to provide technology that might have been used by the military/industrial factions of the Eisenhower administration. These peace-loving, 'human-looking' beings refused to be coopted into the emerging military/industrial complex in the U.S., Britain, Russia and elsewhere on this planet."

But, surprisingly, Casbolt has another treaty story to tell that may be unfamiliar to people reading this book.

"On July 11, 1934, the first treaty with the grays from Orion occurred aboard a naval ship in Balboa, a seaport in Panama," Casbolt claims. "This was one of the most important events in human history because it thrust us into a role we were not prepared for as regards to being a host to a malevolent extraterrestrial race. The U.S. federal government disregarded the Constitution of the United States by doing this and not telling the people. It was here that the agreement was first made between the grays representing the reptilians from Orion and representatives of the U.S. intelligence community."

The 1934 treaty provided for much the same as the alleged agreement of Eisenhower's time, that in return for the grays providing high technology on antigravity, metals and alloys, free energy and medical tech, the government would allow the grays to proceed unhindered with human abductions, but only if a list of abductees was provided and the abductees returned unharmed. In 1944, the second extension of the treaty was signed.

According to Casbolt, the Eisenhower administration signed the third extension of the treaty with the grays in May 1954, three months after the meeting with the Nordics. This third extension was dubbed "The Greada Treaty" and was signed at the Holloman Air Force Base in New Mexico. The original document of the treaty is stored at a National Security Agency facility called "Blue Moon" located under Kirtland Air Force Base, also in New Mexico. The entrance to the base is hidden in the Manzano Mountains, which is also the location for a secret Department of Energy base where free energy devices developed from gray and reptilian technology are being built.

"By the sheer amount of evidence," Casbolt writes, "the only conclusion I can come to is that certain sections of the U.S. and British government have sold us and our children out to malevolent ETs in backdoor treaties. The situation is truly grim. The New World Order and U.N. one-world government are this rigid control structure to clamp the people of the world into a totalitarian vice so they won't have to tell us about the aliens.

"I also believe," he continues, "that certain sections of the intelligence community and the U.S. and British government are directly helping the grays and reptilians with their takeover agenda. Evidence seems to point to the ETs promising these humans certain powers when this happens. The name of the powerful, secretive group, 'The Trilateral Commission,' is taken from the Orion gray/reptilian flag known as the 'Trilateral Insignia.' This shows how much trouble the human race is in."

Casbolt believes – according to secret intelligence documents he claims he has laid eyes on – that the alien harvesting of sperm and egg cells consistently reported by abductees is part of a program intended to genetically "sabotage" the human race, not to peacefully breed a race of hybrids.

"The gray and reptilian agenda," he writes, "is to slowly and covertly take over the planet in the next thirty years, reduce the population and run the planet from underground using the surface population as food to be taken when and how they wish. Although the situation is so horrendous that the governments involved have shattered into panicked factions, some of them have sold out and are directly helping the grays and reptilians."

This is unquestionably a horror movie scenario, but nevertheless various government officials were willing to "sign on the dotted line," possibly in exchange for a privileged position in a post-apocalyptic world.

THE TESTIMONY OF SERGEANT STONE

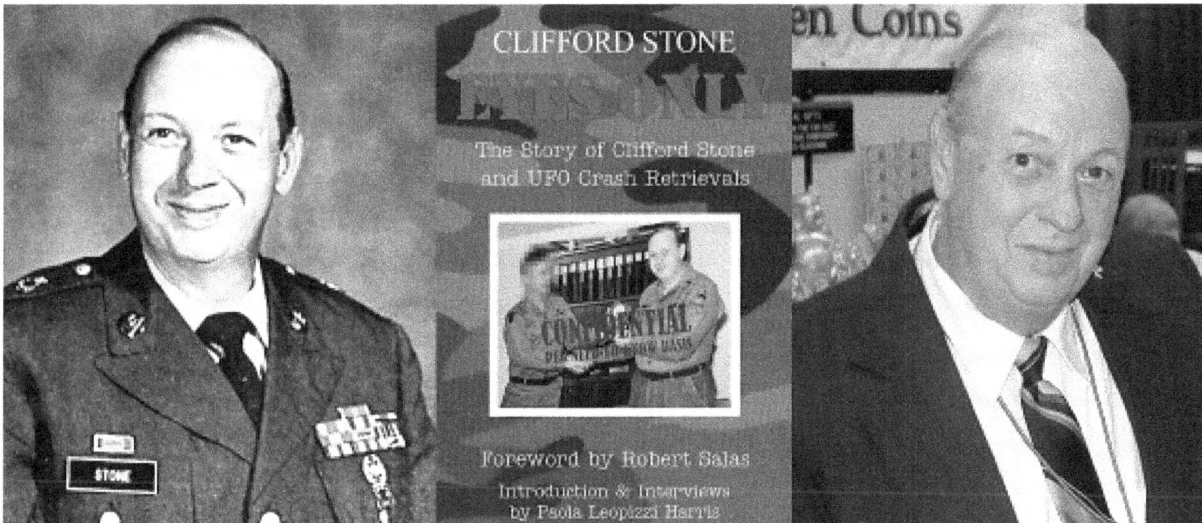

In the spring of 1989, the late lamented magazine "UFO Universe" published an interview with U.S. Army Sergeant Clifford Stone, who at the time was stationed in Roswell, New Mexico. The journalist who conducted the interview, Robert W. Boyajian, begins by making reference to a television special called "UFO Coverup – Live From Washington" on which two mysterious individuals, using the code names "Falcon" and "Condor," spoke of the deal the government had made with the government.

"Essentially, the agreement says that we won't disclose your existence if you won't interfere in our society," Condor said, "and we allow you to operate from a designated base in the United States. It's in the state of Nevada, in an area called Area 51. Extraterrestrials have complete control of the base."

In the main body of the interview, Stone tells Boyajian about how the government came to realize they had made a deal with malevolent aliens.

"Among other things," Stone said, "we agreed that they can have prearranged bases. We will provide security and we will not acknowledge their existence to the general public. In return, they're going to go ahead and carry on certain experimentations, gathering various minerals, getting various flora, various animal life. They're also going to conduct some experiments and research on human beings.

"Now, this troubles us," Stone continued, "because we don't want that to get out of hand, so we bargain a little deeper. We come to the agreement that, okay, if you abduct anyone we need to know who they are so that if there are any problems in the future we can take care of these people, who may need medical or psychological attention, so we can assist with this. They say, fine, we will provide you with a list of all abductees."

The aliens provided the relevant government agencies with lists of 200 or so names every couple of months, but it was discovered that the real number of abductees taken against their will ran into the many thousands. The reasons behind the implanting of alien devices in the abductees were never explained, fueling the disturbing idea that the implants provided some form of total psychological and physical control of the human subject. Stone also discussed the idea that the abductees were being warned that they had been given information that they would recall at a preset time in the future and that they would be expected to act on when the time came.

Is there any way to prevent some sort of alien control of the Earth's population?

"The U.S. government may believe that there's no defense," Stone said, "and that the aliens are highly evolved and technologically superior to us. There are those of us, however, that firmly believe – or should I say 'know' – that there are defenses against these folks. In unity there is strength. That strength is derived from knowledge. The knowledge that must be had is knowledge of the truth. With the truth, we can go ahead and combat these entities."

WILLIAM COOPER'S "PETITION TO INDICT"

Finding a legal and aboveboard method of resisting alien control was also the goal of the aforementioned William Cooper, who drafted a document called the "Petition to Indict" that one can still find posted on the Internet.

The document begins by saying, "The government of these United States of America, having been formed under the Constitution and having been duly elected and appointed by the people of these United States of America under the terms of the Constitution, has violated the public trust, terms, conditions and laws of the land as outlined and enshrined within the Constitution of these United States of America.

"To Wit:

AMERICA'S TOP SECRET TREATY WITH ALIEN LIFE FORMS

(1) The government has approved and entered into a secret treaty with an Alien Nation against the terms of the Constitution and without the advice and consent of the Congress or the people.

(2) The government in this treaty has given this Alien Nation land and bases within the borders of these United States of America.

(3) The government in this treaty has traded human lives and property for the alien technology and has denied the citizens of these United States of America the lawful protection due them under the Constitution. The property is in the form of livestock and land.

(4) [In all the foregoing] this Alien Nation has proved to be the mortal enemy of the people, the nation and all of humanity. Abductions, surgical operations, implantations, biological sampling, impregnations, psychological damage and other horrors have been and are being performed upon humans by this Alien Nation. For these reasons, a state of war now exists and has existed between the people of the United States and this Alien Nation."

Cooper goes on to charge the government with conspiracy, murder and treason against the people and the Constitution. He also says that in the process of aiding and abetting the Alien Nation in the performance of these crimes against the people, the nation and humanity, the government, with full knowledge and consent, has murdered, incarcerated, forcibly relocated, brainwashed, drugged, harassed and otherwise interfered unlawfully in the lives of "patriots," including a U.S. president, who have attempted to expose this murder and treason.

Like the MI6 agent, James Casbolt, quoted earlier in this chapter, Cooper accuses the government of financing its alien agenda through the importation and sale of illegal narcotics to the American people, especially the country's youth. He singles out the CIA as the main instrument in the control of the world's drug market. The intelligence agencies' rationale for this heinous distribution of illegal narcotics, according to Cooper, is that it will "identify and eliminate the weak elements of our society."

Article nine of Cooper's petition calls for the impeachment of then president George Bush. Bush was a member of MJ-12 (a secret postwar government council convened to deal with the alien question) and served with the Trilateral Commission. Bush, it is claimed, also organized and has headed the narcotics smuggling conspiracy since its beginning.

"We firmly believe," the document continues, "that George Bush now heads this shadow government that controls the Alien technology, the military-industrial complex and thus the nation. The fact that he is now the President of the United States of America makes George Bush the most powerful and dangerous criminal in the history of the world."

The document also calls for full pardons in exchange for full disclosure, meaning that those who speak publicly about their role in the conspiracy should be promised immunity from prosecution for any criminal acts committed in service to the Alien alliance. But for those who persist in this conspiracy of murder and treason, no mercy should be shown.

"We charge the government to cease all conspiracies, operations, projects, treaties and any other involvement with this Alien Nation. We charge the government to order this Alien Nation and all of its members to leave the United States and this Earth immediately, now and for all time, and we charge the government to enforce this order. We further charge the government to make a complete disclosure of its alien conspiracy to the American people and to make a full accounting of its actions. We charge the Congress to order this to be done and we charge the Congress to enforce this order."

In the petition, which was published sometime around 1989, Cooper and the undersigned promised to fight to bring the guilty parties to justice, saying they will persist until their deaths to accomplish these ends in the name of humanity.

In a sense, Cooper did fight his alien/government conspiracy battles to the death. As he moved away from the mainstream UFO community and gravitated in the direction of the militia and anti-government subculture in the late 1990s, he came to believe he had been personally targeted by President Bill Clinton and the IRS. Cooper was charged with income tax evasion in 1998, and a warrant for his arrest was issued. He eluded repeated attempts to serve the warrant and in 2000 was named a "major fugitive" by the United States Marshalls.

On November 5, 2001, Apache County sheriff's deputies attempted to arrest Cooper at his Eager, Arizona, home on charges of aggravated assault with a deadly weapon and endangerment. The charges stemmed from Cooper's disputes with some local residents. After an exchange of gunfire during which Cooper shot one of the deputies in the head, Cooper was himself fatally shot. Federal authorities said at the time that Cooper had spent years evading execution of the 1998 arrest warrant and had vowed that "he would not be taken alive." He may have been "tilting with windmills" in regard to the conspiracy, but one of the windmills shot back.

In any case, Cooper's "Petition to Indict" does directly and specifically lay out the particulars of why the government's alleged signed treaty with malevolent gray aliens was unconstitutional. But the notion that simply and honestly bringing the problem before Congress would force disclosure and openness about a conspiracy that reached to the highest heights of the government of the United States and the other major world powers is naïve and wishful thinking.

AMERICA'S TOP SECRET TREATY WITH ALIEN LIFE FORMS

DOES CHINA ALSO HAVE A DEAL WITH THE ALIENS?

In a posting on a website dedicated to Canadian UFO contactee Oscar Magosci, writer Joe Daniels offers up another story of alleged government dealings with the aliens, this time the Chinese.

"Threatened by recent East-West relations," Daniels writes, "and the revolutionary movements within itself, China is preparing for the final ideological war. The aliens have agreed to defend China from the free world's combined military and nuclear forces."

Meanwhile, China is arming the Middle East with their own nuclear arsenals. Unifying the Arabs under the one Chinese command was simple, Daniels claims, especially given Israel's "iron fist" attitude toward the occupied territories.

Soviet warheads were sent to Syria onboard a UFO, with the use of Soviet nukes instead of Chinese weapons being part of a disinformation campaign to sabotage U.S. relations with Russia. The Russian warheads were hijacked from Soviet subs in the Dragon's Triangle, which is an alien-controlled section of the Pacific Ocean once frequented by the Russian navy. After losing some 900 high-yield warheads and 13 vessels, commanders were ordered to steer clear of the area.

The rather convoluted story continues by saying that the most important alien tech is two-millimeter, spheroid brain implants which are surgically inserted through the nasal orifice and into the brain, ensuring that an individual can be fully monitored and controlled. Such mind slave experiments have long been supported by the U.S. and Canadian governments and apparently are also part of the psychological weaponry of China. The people so implanted are called "zombies" and have been programmed to help with the overthrow of mankind in the near future.

When China finishes with its plans to subdue the Middle East, it will invade Europe. At the same time, Chinese space-based bacteriological weapons will be launched at the Arctic. The winds will carry the airborne diseases into Russia and North America. In days, hundreds of millions will be dead and survivors will be at the mercy of the Chinese, the aliens and the zombies.

The aliens want this all-out war to minimize human resistance when they invade. They tried using this method before with Nazi Germany. Many of the scientific advances of today came from German science which had itself been based on alien technology. Had Hitler won the war, the Earth would have become one huge concentration camp in order to depopulate the continents for the aliens.

Why do the aliens seem to so much need our world? According to Daniels, the aliens preceded man on the evolutionary scale by millions of years and had been created at the time of the dinosaurs. Some 67.5 million years ago an interdimensional war destroyed most of their civilization and forced them to leave the Earth. Now they have chosen to reclaim what was once theirs.

THE FATEFUL TOOTH OF TIME

This chapter started with a simple trip to the dentist for President Dwight Eisenhower. Or so we, the American public, were told.

How could anyone have suspected that lurking behind that fateful tooth was a conspiracy to conquer, enslave and ultimately destroy the human race? Using the Trojan horse of promises of advanced technology, the hostile gray aliens insinuated themselves into the lives of every American citizen – all the while concealing a coldhearted mission of completely subduing a purportedly free people.

And they even got it from us in writing! One is reminded about the old joke, "Be sure to read the fine print at the bottom."

Whatever the details of this insidious treaty, no matter what was agreed to, what egregious concessions were made, no matter who profited or was enriched, it is we who will pay the final price of that ill-conceived diplomatic outreach to a dark alien race from the stars.

Did the U.S. sign a treaty with a group of aliens? If so, what were the aliens' ulterior motives, and how has the Treaty worked out over the years?

A HIDDEN TIME LINE – PART ONE

1) The purpose of this document is to provide humanity with information about hidden threats that exist to the free will and self-determination of mankind. This information describes threats from extraterrestrial societies, international organizations, and domestic shadow government activities. The implications of successful fruition of these threats are also presented along with information that must be considered when planning a strategy for resisting these threats and ultimate objectives.

2) This document attempts to expose the fact that all three sources of threats must be considered together because they are all interrelated. What may appear to be independent groups with vastly different agendas are all actually working toward the same goal of world domination and the abolishment of individual freedom for all of mankind. The only way to prevent this from happening is for humanity to become aware of the threats and respond as one people, despite how unpleasant this may be. It is morally improper to remain silent and do nothing to prevent global domination from occurring.

3) This document contains information of a serious and troubling nature that will be emotionally disturbing to sensitive individuals. Only by viewing this information from a dispassionate and discerning point of view, can the emotional reactions of anger, fear, anxiety, and depression be avoided. This document may not represent all truths from all points of view. It only presents information relevant to

the preservation of Human freedom.

4) This document provides a full operational briefing. However, it only contains a summary of available information. For a better understanding of the topics covered herein, the reader is encouraged to review the source material listed in the References section. Each section, subsection, and paragraph of this document is assigned individual numbers for identification in regards to source references that are listed in section 7. For instance, "2.3.4" refers to the fourth subsection of the third subsection of the second main section of the document.

5) Every paragraph within each section is also sequentially numbered, such as this paragraph of "5)". In addition, the Reference section identifies portions of paragraphs with a fractional percentage number after a decimal point. For instance, "2.5" indicates the mid point of the second paragraph and "3.9" indicates the bottom of the third paragraph. By using the section and paragraph numbers, the source of all information presented in this document can be determined by finding the associated numbers that are listed sequentially in the References section.

Ancient History

1) In order to understand the nature of the threats facing humanity, it is necessary to know what events have taken place that have brought us to the point of where we are today. This section describes the origins of modern civilizations and the affects that extraterrestrials have had upon human development. The next section will cover important events that have occurred in recent history that have brought us to where we are today.

2) 75 million years ago, an Intergalactic Federation existed, consisting of 75 planetary civilizations. However, this Federation was overcome by a catastrophe resulting in a cultural desert with fragmentation, over population, and war. 50 million years ago, Tall Blond entities from the Andromeda Galaxy used a black hole to enter the Milky Way Galaxy near Arcturus. They settled in the Lyran system. 22 million years ago, the Lyran wars began. Portions of the Lyran population settled in the Orion, Taurus, and Era constellations.

3) On Earth, early human development evolved slowly for the first 150 million years. Then, two million years ago, the Elohim came to Earth from the Aldebaran System. They were a tall humanoid species with blond hair and fair skin. They departed with over 10,000 of our simian ancestors. Hundreds of years later, they returned to deposit a more advanced, genetically engineered race that could use tool and fire. The Elohim have returned seven times within a period of 23,000 years to accelerate human evolution. 450,000 years ago, the Anunnaki settled on Earth from the planet Nibiru at Mesopotamia.

4) 300,000 years ago, a great civil war began on Rigel, within the Orion constellation. Peaceful tall Blonds escaped to the Procyon system in Canis Minor.

Those who remained on Rigel became the tall Grays with genetic damage due to the nuclear weapons exchange. 208,000 years ago, the tall Grays reconstituted their power base and began the Markab Empire with the short Grays from Betelgeuses and conquered Procyon covertly with mind control.

5) 100,000 years ago, the Anunnaki mated with Neanderthal beings to form Cro-Magnon terrestrial beings as a genetic hybrid for mining purposes. 70,000 years ago, Lemuria and Atlantian civilizations began to flourish. 50,000 years ago, 70,000 rebellious beings left the Pleiades and settled on Earth where they flourished. 40,000 years ago, war broke out. Nearly all on Earth were destroyed. A few escaped to another planet. The Survivors on Earth became wild and degenerated. 35,000 years ago, those who had escaped, returned and rebuilt Lemuria and Atlantis.

6) 30,000 years ago, the current Homo Sapiens began in the Andes. 12,000 years ago, Lemuria and Atlantis are destroyed by global catastrophes. 6,000 years ago, the Sumer civilization thrived between the Tigris and Euphrates Rivers of present day Iraq. 5,000 years ago, civilizations spread to Europe and the Indus Valley of India.

HIDDEN TIME LINE – PART TWO

1) In 1776, a secret organization was started by a Jesuit priest named Adam Weishaupt. This organization was known as the Order of the Illuminati. Its purpose was to take over political control from the Catholic Church and the Kings of Europe. In 1777, Adam Weishaupt was initiated into the Masonic Order in Munich, Germany.

2) On January 25, 1878, farmer John Mertin of Dallas, Texas observed a flying disc. On August 12, 1889, Jose Bonilla took several pictures of over 300 objects which crossed the Sun. In 1896 and on into 1897, a wave of sightings occurred in the United States of winged cigar shaped craft and airships. In 1909, the first recorded wave of European sightings occurred in England.

3) In 1932, Adolph Hitler directed German scientists to work on aircraft designs using advanced technology provided by Gray entities from inside the Earth. In 1933, Franklin D. Roosevelt became President of the United States. Roosevelt was a Mason at the time when interaction with the Gray entities began with the U.S. Government. In the winter of 1933-34, there were 487 flying disk-sighting cases in Scandinavia (240 Norway, 96 Sweden, 157 Finland).

4) On July 11, 1934, aboard a naval ship in Balboa, the first deal was made between the United States and the Grays. The agreement stated that the aliens would not interfere in our affairs and we would not interfere in their affairs. It allowed the aliens to establish underground bases on U.S. soil in exchange for alien technology.

5) During the winter of 1936-37, there was another wave of increased

sightings of disks over Scandinavia. In 1938, the Germans began flying experimental craft using unconventional power sources and Methods obtained from a downed alien craft. Also in 1938, the U.S. Government engaged Orson Wells to do the "War of the Worlds" broadcast in order to gauge public reaction to the idea of alien contact.

6) In 1947, a powerful radar unit caused the crash of several alien disks in the Four Corners area of the U.S. The most notable of which were at Roswell and Aztec, New Mexico. The disks recovered had a reptilian species on board as well as the bodies of U.S. Air Force pilots that had been mutilated. The disk crash at Roswell netted one live alien that was referred to as EBE for Extra-terrestrial Biological Entity.

7) President Truman knew nothing about aliens prior to this time. He responded quickly to keep everything about the aliens secret and established a group of 12 top military and scientific personnel to deal with the aliens. They were known as the Majestic-12 and the group still exists today with different representatives.

8) In September of 1947, President Truman caused the National Security Act to be passed, creating the Central Intelligence Agency, in order to hide the activities of the government and the alien problem. CIA mind control projects began at Bethesda Naval Hospital. Project Sign was created on December 30, 1947 at Wright Field to investigate disk technology capabilities and performance. The Navy Auxiliary Field in the Groom Mountains of Nevada was chosen as the place to do the testing.

9) In 1949, alien craft were often seen hovering over sensitive nuclear installations, especially in New Mexico. Probes, known as "green fireballs", were frequently seen over the state. In 1949, another disk crashed, with one fatality and one living alien that was kept in a facility with an electromagnetic grid. In December of 1950, a disk crashed in the El Indio-Guerro area of Mexico and was taken to the AEC facility at Sandia in New Mexico. In 1951, flying wing type aircraft were seen over Albuquerque.

10) Also in 1951, the alien, known as EBE, suddenly became ill and died in 1952. In 1952, President Truman created the National Security Agency to monitor and contain the secret of the alien presence, decipher alien communications, and eventually establish an ongoing dialog with any aliens it could communicate with.

11) In 1952, a group known as the Bilderbergers was created in order to take the decision making about the alien problem and other international issues out of the hands of governments. The Bilderbergers, headquartered in Geneva, evolved into an elite secret body that still controls international situations.

12) In July of 1952, disks flew over Washington D.C., creating a public stir. One of the disks flew away at a speed estimated at over 7,300 mph. In 1953, there

were 10 disk crashes, 26 dead and 4 living aliens. Astronomers in 1953, discovered a large object that entered the solar system and later proved to be intelligently guided and emitted communication signals. The Air Force, in the same year, discovered huge orbiting objects between 100 to 500 miles in altitude. They were alien craft.

13) In 1953, members of the Pleiadian race met with President Eisenhower to warn him about the Grays and offer their help. But, to receive their help, the people of the planet would have to stop killing each other, stop polluting and destroying the Earth, and request their help as one people. Their help was refused because they would not provide advanced technology.

14) It was decided by the government to communicate with the Grays and possibly acquire advanced technology. They also wanted to find out more about both the aliens and the role they were playing in mutilations and abductions of humans and animals. Project Sigma, a joint NSA/CIA project to communicate with the alien species, was successful. The aliens told the government that their abductions of humans were for medical examination purposes only.

15) Diplomatic relations were established and a meeting was held between elements of the U.S. government and the Grays from the Marcab Empire on April 25, 1954 at 6pm at Holloman AFB. Two disks hovered above the runway while a third landed. Representatives of each species were exchanged. The representative of the EBAN, as they call themselves, was named Krlll (no vowels) and confined to an Electro-magnetically secure facility near Los Alamos.

16) A secret treaty was negotiated with the EBAN by the United States government. The agreement was made and contained some of the following provisions: (1) The U.S. would not reveal the alien presence and would not interfere with alien operations, (2) The U.S. would allow the aliens to maintain underground bases on U.S. soil, (3) The U.S. would allow the aliens to abduct it's citizens on a periodic and limited basis for medical examination, provided that the people were returned unharmed and without memory of the interaction, (4) The aliens would furnish a periodic list of abductees to the NSC, and (5) The aliens would provide the U.S. with advanced technology.

17) To finance these "Black" projects, without being accountable to the U.S. Congress, the government allowed Lucky Luciano to return to Italy in 1949. Heroin began flowing into the United States in the 1950's. Today, the U.S. government is the largest purchaser and distributor of heroin and cocaine in the world. Primarily, the CIA and the Delta security forces (sponsored by the NRO) were involved.

18) By April of 1954, the U.S. began to suspect that the aliens were abducting a larger number of people than were being reported to the NSC. They realized that they had made an error in trusting the aliens. The purposes for the abductions turned out to be: (1) Insertion of an implant device for the biological

monitoring, tracking, and control of the abductee, (2) Implementation of a post hypnotic suggestion to carry out a specific activity during a specific time period, (3) Termination of some people for biological materials and substances, (4) Termination of individuals who represented a threat to their activities, (5) Effect genetic engineering experiments, and (6) Impregnation of human females for the creation of crossbred infants.

19) So, the aliens had violated the agreement. The government realized that there was little that they could do but try to keep the information classified to prevent panic. It became increasingly obvious to MJ-12 that things were not going as planned. The extent and number of persons reported missing every year is a closely guarded government secret. But since 1980, there have been at least 20,000 children reported missing each year. There have been over 14,000 cattle mutilations since 1973. And, over 20 million Americans have reported seeing a UFO.

20) In 1955, a large donut shaped UFO was seen over New York. In 1956, mind control experiments on prison inmates, was approved in the United States. On August 13, 1956, radar operators at RAF Bentwaters, England, detected objects flying over the North Sea at a speed of 4,000 mph.

21) In March of 1956, at the White Sands Missile Range in New Mexico, Air Force sergeant Jonathan P. Lovette, was abducted by aliens. An Air Force major witnessed him being hauled aboard a flying disk with tentacle-like cables. His mutilated body was found three days later about ten miles from where it was taken.

22) In 1957, a facility code named DREAMLAND, was constructed at Groom Lake, Nevada in the proximity of an alien underground base known as S-4. The bargained for technology was set in place but could only be operated by the aliens themselves. It was found that the advanced technology could not be used against the aliens, should the need arise.

23) In 1961, Cape Canaveral/Kennedy radar locked onto an object that was following a Polaris missile over the ocean. Vice President Johnson's private aircraft crashed. Radar showed UFOs in the area. At Fort Ord, California, 221 military members were abducted and implanted with devices. All were sedated through the efforts of 600 other soldiers who were recruited for the purpose and debriefed. Many suffered severe physical and psychological trauma. They and their families were sequestered.

24) On September 21st of 1961, two Boeing 707s encountered a large donut shaped UFO over the Pacific Ocean. Betty and Barney Hill were abducted in New Hampshire. The Hills were taken onboard a disk, examined, and released with memory loss until it was later revealed under hypnosis. Also in 1961, President Kennedy, dissatisfied with some areas in the covert government structure, threatened to go public about the alien presence.

25) In 1962, the Bilderbergers met to discuss the ultimatum. 1962 was also the year that a space probe landed on Mars and confirmed the presence of a viable atmosphere. Disk activity was observed by the public around Dulce, New Mexico, which was the site of a joint government-alien underground facility.

26) In 1963, mind control experiments began in Warminster, England. In May of 1963, Gordon Cooper had visual contact with a UFO while in orbit on a Mercury flight. Within a month after President Kennedy's assassination, the Bilderbergers met again to formulate their plans.

27) In April of 1964, Cape Kennedy radar technicians tracked disks in pursuit of a Gemini capsule. On April 15th, two intelligence personnel met with aliens in the New Mexico desert to arrange a meeting on April 25th at Holloman AFB, New Mexico in order to solve the problems with the Grays.

28) In 1966, the Soviet Union had a massive wave of sightings. In October of 1967, Britain was hit by a wave of disk sightings. In 1968, disks that were known to be flown by the U.S. Navy, were frequently seen around China Lake, California. In May of 1968, disks frequented the demilitarized zone in Viet Nam.

29) On July 20-21 1969, the Apollo 11 crew witnessed a huge alien spacecraft surround their landing site on the moon. In October of 1969, Jimmy Carter reported seeing a UFO. A major flap of spacecraft sightings occurred in Australia.

30) In late 1972 and early 1973, numerous sightings of disks occurred in South Africa, Latin America, Eastern Europe, Canada, and in Australia. On October 25, 1973, a disk buzzed the National Security Agency High-frequency transmitter facility at NW Cape in Western Australia. In 1974, large numbers of animal mutilations began to occur in Texas.

31) In 1975, captured German technology allowed development of a sonic weapon against the EBEs. The project continued until 1978. In November of 1975, Travis Walton was abducted and returned five days later. Also in 1975, bases in the northern tier of the U.S., were flown over by UFOs. Chase planes lost them near New Brunswick, Canada.

32) In 1977, President Carter was elected and said that he would make every piece of information about UFOs available to the public. Carter was shown a disk and changed his mind. In 1978, a wave of sightings in England began that lasted until 1983 with some 3,000 sightings documented. On March 18, 1978, William Herman was abducted and told by the aliens of the existence of a "network" of civilizations.

33) In September 1978, scientist Paul Bennewitz discovered the activities of alien craft at Manzano Weapons Storage area outside of Albuquerque, New Mexico. In November 1978, a huge cylindrical object was seen hovering over oil company equipment in Kuwait. The CIA had secured control over most of the worldwide traffic in opium by the end of 1978.

34) 1979 was the year that a disgruntled scientist at the Dulce Bio-Genetics Facility fled with evidence, vowing to expose the atrocities found there. In October 1979, 66 people were killed during an altercation with aliens at the underground facility near Dulce, N.M. Also in 1979, Electronic Identification Research began at Los Alamos National Labs for identification implants.

35) In 1980, the Federal Emergency Management Agency conducted REX-80, readiness exercises in which they relocated Cuban refugees as part of a population relocation test. In May of 1980, Myrna Hanson related information, under hypnosis, of being abducted and taken to an underground base with vats. Also in May, Judy Doraty and her son witnessed a cattle mutilation and were abducted and implanted themselves. In December of 1980, the Cash-Landrum incident occurred where both women received severe radiation poisoning during an encounter with a U.S. disk.

36) In 1982, the Federal Emergency Management Agency conducted the REX-82 exercise, which tested the nation's ability to mobilize quickly for wartime military production. Industry failed miserably. In 1983, FEMA obtains standby legislation with the passing of the "Defense Resources Act". This bill suspends the Bill of Rights, abolishes free enterprise, eliminates privately owned property, and censors all means of communication in the event that a National Emergency is declared under any pretext.

37) On April 26, 1984, General Bond is killed while flying in Area 51 during a classified aerial test. In September of that year, a high delta-winged craft soundlessly buzzed golfers in Australia, which set Royal Australian Air Force into motion. The event caused the subject of UFOs to be raised in Parliament.

38) In September of 1987, 16-cycle waves are broadcast for a period of four months before the election of George Bush. The ELF waves caused entrainment of millions of Americans to occur. On September 21, 1987, President Reagan voiced his thoughts about aliens threatening the Earth in an address to the United Nations. On the 27th of November, groups of U.S. Army Rangers attempted, but apparently bungled, to enter a joint U.S.-alien facility in New Mexico.

39) On December 17, 1987, a UFO in Gulf Breeze, Florida dropped a fluid on the local athletic field. Analysis showed that the fluid was of unknown origin. In 1988, George Bush became President. A joint U.S.-alien base off the Florida coast was reactivated, giving rise to the sightings at Gulf Breeze.

40) In May of 1988, Ronald Reagan again made a speech in which he referred to an "alien threat from outside this world". In New Mexico, an antimatter weapon was developed at Los Alamos as a weapon of last resort if "the Grays cannot be pried away from the planet". The number of Grays on Earth was estimated at 20 million.

41) In February of 1989, the government began communications with a Rep-

tilian species (who were advancing on this system), because they were one of the few enemies of the Grays who could get rid of them.

42) In 1989, data on Project Excaliber was released. The project was involved in developing a warhead that would penetrate 1,000 meters of earth and then detonate. This was useful for destroying underground bases. On May 7th, the South Africans shot down a flying disk. U.S. pilots exited the craft and South Africa complained about invasion of their airspace. On June 30th, after a spree of what were possibly government induced violent episodes with guns on school yards, gun legislation was presented to Congress to disarm the American public.

43) On October 11, 1989, a large disk was seen by hundreds of witnesses in eastern Oklahoma. Sightings began to be reported in Iowa and around the U.S. in large numbers. On October 16, 1989, information was disclosed about a disagreement between the U.S. and Soviet Union in a base on the far side of the Moon in which several U.S. scientists were machine-gunned in 1986 or 1987.

44) In January of 1990, witnesses in Lancaster, California viewed a delta shaped craft, 900 feet long, fly slowly over a ten minute period. The craft was accompanied by another disk. On February 17th, a Ukrainian astronomer detected radio emissions near Altair, which has been associated with reptilian creatures.

45) In 1994, the motion picture film of an alien autopsy in 1947 was released. In 1997, the failed attempt to shoot down an alien spacecraft in space, was videotaped from the Space Shuttle, and released to the public. In 1998, the videotaped evidence of UFO activity, from several people all over the world, were released. Also in 1998, many of the original MJ-12 documents were released. In 1999, the first national televised presentation about UFOs occurred during prime time, with "Confirmation, The Hard Evidence".

HIDDEN TIME LINE – PART THREE

1) Across from a giant radio telescope at Chilbolton in England, a crop formation appeared in a wheat field on August 19, 2001. It was 75 feet wide and 120 feet long. It contained a response to a message that we humans sent out into space back in November of 1974. Dr. Carl Segan and Francis Drake created the message as part of the project for the search of extraterrestrial intelligence.

2) It was transmitted with two trillion watts of radiated energy from the Arecibo radio telescope in Puerto Rico. The message was sent in a very narrow beam towards a galactic cluster known as M13, which is 65 million light years away. It was a pictogram arranged in a matrix of 23 pixels by 73 pixels. It was intended to describe our numbering system, the building blocks and formulas for DNA, a double helix symbol of DNA, a figure of a human being, our solar system, and a diagram of the radio telescope that sent the message.

3) The crop formation looked very similar to the Arecibo message with some very interesting differences. Below the dot pattern for our numbering system, the

crop formation had an additional pattern that indicated the atomic number of Silicon in addition to the hydrogen, carbon, nitrogen, oxygen, and phosphorus numbers, which are the basic elements for life on this planet. Instead of a double helix symbol of DNA, the crop formation depicted three sets of diagonal lines that indicate three strands of DNA.

4) Instead of a depiction of a human being, as presented in the Arecibo message, the crop pattern had a different depiction of a humanoid form. This new depiction showed a body with two arms and legs like humans. But, the head was much larger. The height of the crop formation's body was indicated as being a little taller than half our height. And, the dot pattern in the crop formation indicated a population that was almost six and a half billion larger than our own.

5) The Arecibo message depicted the 9 planets around the Sun with the symbol for Earth raised above the rest to indicate where humanity lives. Earth's dot was also located directly below the depiction of man. In the crop formation, there were three symbols that were raised above the rest. They indicated the planets of Earth, Mars, and Nibiru. However, it was the symbol for Mars that was located directly below the humanoid body.

6) At the very bottom of both formations, you have distinctly different dot patterns. The Arecibo message had a depiction of the telescope that sent the message with an indicated size of 2,430. The crop formation had a depiction of something else with a size of 6,748. It was very similar to another crop formation of one year earlier in the very same wheat field that depicted a new form of radiated energy.

7) If the information presented is accurate, we now know that we are not alone in the universe. There is intelligent life on Mars and on the planet Nibiru. We know the general form and size of what they look like, the composition of their DNA, and their population. We also know how they communicate and, most importantly, that they want to communicate with us. But, what this formation does not tell us is why they want to communicate with us and share their advanced technology or what their intentions may be.

HIDDEN TIME LINE – PART FOUR

1) On August 15th of 2002, an elaborate crop formation was discovered at Crabwood Farm House in Winchester County, England. It was a framed design of an extraterrestrial being holding out a disk that measured 232 feet by 390 feet. The disk was 100 feet in diameter. The head appeared to be large with a pointed chin, parted mouth, small nose, and large eyes. It had a long neck and thin torso. There were also three small shapes in the background that appeared to be UFOs.

2) This crop formation had a much higher resolution quality than the facial crop formation of one year earlier. That is because horizontal lines of varying widths

were used, which is the same way that pictures are displayed in television.

3) The disk was composed of blocks formed by standing crops surrounded by flattened crops. It was a spiral pattern with a sequence of blocks and spaces that started in the center and spiraled out to the edge of the disk. The sequence was divided into groups of eight equal parts that were separated by triangular arrowhead-shaped symbols. The patterns represented letters and symbols, based upon a computer code known as ASCII, which actually spelled out an intelligent message.

4) The complete translation of the message on the disk stated, "Beware the bearers of FALSE gifts & their BROKEN PROMISES. Much PAIN but still time. BELIEVE. There is GOOD out there. We oppose DECEPTION. Conduit CLOSING,". All of the letters in some of the words were all capitalized in order to add emphasis.

5) The first sentence states, "Beware the bearers of FALSE gifts & their BROKEN PROMISES." This message is far too important to simply be telling us to be cautious of one another. Because this message appears to be of extraterrestrial origin, it appears to be referring to the intentions of an alien race that could offer us advanced technology and spiritual guidance. Although it does not specifically reveal whether false gifts have been offered in the past or will be offered in the future, it does say that those who offer the gifts have broken their promises in the past. This is telling us that we should be suspicious of any gifts from an alien race and that we should not trust everything that they tell us.

6) The second sentence says, "Much PAIN but still time." Whoever wrote this is displaying compassion for human suffering, which they know exists on this planet. Although this does not indicate who is suffering, it can be assumed that the pain referred to here is caused by the bearers of false gifts and broken promises. However, it does state that there is still time to overcome the pain.

7) The next sentence consists of a single word, "BELIEVE." It is telling us to believe that there is still time for humanity to end the suffering here. This is calling for a huge leap of faith by all of humanity to trust the authors of this message, have hope, and believe that there is still time to overcome the pain.

8) The next sentence states, "There is GOOD out there." It implies that there are good entities that can help to stop the pain. Although there is no indication of immediate help, it is saying that there are good entities that can help us.

9) The next sentence states, "We oppose DECEPTION." This identifies the source of this message as coming from a group of beings that are concerned about the dangers to humanity by untrustworthy entities that seek to deceive us with false gifts. They are making it clear that it is their intention to oppose those who would take advantage of others through deception.

10) The last sentence is the most puzzling. It states, "Conduit CLOSING."

AMERICA'S TOP SECRET TREATY WITH ALIEN LIFE FORMS

There is no mention as to what the conduit is used for or why we should be interested in the fact that it is closing. A conduit is a channel that enables fluids, cables, and other materials to pass through it. It is also defined as a narrow corridor for people to pass between buildings. In the context of this message, this may be referring to a passageway or portal that enables entities to pass into our world. The fact that it is closing could be telling us that no more entities can come into our world or leave. However, the message ends with a comma, which indicates that the last sentence is incomplete and that there is more information to follow.

HIDDEN TIME LINE — THREAT ASSESSMENT

1) This section is intended to identify threats to human freedom and assess the level of severity that they pose to mankind. The threats are differentiated according to their areas of influence for being foreign, international, and individual. This differentiation is only for organizational purposes. It must be noted that all of the threats are interrelated with a common malevolent goal of world domination.

2) The subsection relating to "Foreign Threats" presents information about extraterrestrial societies that have come to Earth. The origins, physiology, motives and current activities of each species, is described in detail. The subsection relating to "International Threats" presents information about secret societies, both global and regional, as well as satanic cults. The subsection on "Individual Threats" describes government sponsored covert projects in the areas of drugs, mind control, terrorism, and national security.

3) Mankind has suffered from a form of darkness for most of its history. The Creator Source is Love and Light and is incapable of generating such a hideous form of energy. Creation, in order to create, has a positive and negative polarity. There are Beings of Light in both sides of the energy forms that make up the whole. The Beings on the negative pole play an important part in Creation. Without it, Creation could not exist.

4) When Beings wished to create, they were instructed that they must go to their Creator in order to receive the light and energy in the form of love so that anything created would follow its evolutionary path to higher states of consciousness. However, eons ago, some of these Beings of the negative polarity decided that they could create with their own energy. They created clones of themselves, which took on a life of their own. They have no soul light from the Creator. They began multiplying and replicating themselves.

5) This is the face of evil. It has been termed the Luciferian consciousness. However, evil is known among the Galactic star nations by another more accurate term: Artificial Replicating Viral Intelligence or ARVI for short. The visiting negative, malevolent 'astronaut gods' of long ago were physical, replicating strains of ARVI. This includes all of the abnormal Grays and Reptilian lines of malevolent alien life forms.

6) These Beings learned how to tap into the light bodies of beings in different galaxies. They would suck the life out of them. They grew enormous in their appetite. They designed implants and ways of controlling beings so that they were enslaved like herds of cattle to be milked whenever their light was needed.

7) ARVI needs to keep beings in a state of fear. Fear leaches light from Human Beings through the cordings and implants that are attached to most people. ARVI created a huge storage supply system to keep stores of light energy. The cordings and implants are connected to this vast storage system.

8) This is the reason for the kidnapping and brutalizing of so many humans, where ruthless experiments are visited upon these people. DNA, both human and animal, is harvested in order to keep replicating the various ARVI strains. Any abduction that is forced upon humans, which is disrespectful and in denial of free will, is perpetrated by ARVI strains.

9) ARVI has human servants/hosts that are rewarded when they perform acts of evil by feeding the host/ego plenty of money and power. All wants and desires are fulfilled. But, if a servant rebels, then ARVI destroys it. This is how human sacrifice began on Earth. The viral intelligence (Luciferian consciousness) was a fearful demonic god that demanded to be fed blood. In turn, it would not bring violence to a tribe. Blood sacrifice is still being offered up to ARVI through violence, hatred, war and greed.

10) ARVI has been clever in convincing some of humanity that it is part of the family of souls that the Creator created. ARVI strains can appear to be very loving on the surface. Real Beings have been duped into making agreements and contracts to give ARVI the DNA that it needs in order to keep replicating itself.

11) The story that some of the Grays tell of their star system collapsing and needing help from Earth is not true. These ARVI strains take advantage of human compassion in order to dupe people into cooperating with them, believing that they are assisting space brothers at a time of need. Let it be known that all such contracts can and should be voided.

HIDDEN TIME LINE – PART FIVE

1) The universe is immense and full of life. Intelligent life is concentrated in some places more than others. There is a great diversity of life in the galaxy. Our world exists in an area of congregation with many inhabited worlds. Our world is being scrutinized by many powerful forces.

2) Societies exist in the universe at every conceivable level of social and spiritual development and in countless expressions. There are vast areas that are unexplored and sparsely populated where many societies live in secret. Many have never been discovered.

3) The universe is a rigorous existence for survival. It is a difficult and com-

petitive environment. It is not a heavenly state. Everyone in the universe must deal with the rigors of physical life of survival, hardship, competition, and depravation.

4) There are many civilizations and empires that are far older than humanity. Wars and great conflicts do occur in the universe, but they are very rare. Resources are valuable and so, the destruction of resources is generally looked upon with disfavor. Rebellions and internal disputes are more common. It is better to persuade a race to come into alliance with you than to try to overtake them by force. So, advanced nations have become powerful in influencing mental environments.

5) As societies become more technologically advanced, the need for resources becomes greater and the preservation of natural resources is emphasized. In many cases, home worlds have outstripped their resources to where they have become barren and unproductive. That is why Earth is viewed with such great interest. It is rich in mineral and biological resources, strategically located, and accessible to many civilizations.

6) Fortunately for us, our world cannot be conquered, for we live in a region that is governed by rules of conduct. This means that our world cannot become apart of a larger association unless humanity visibly demonstrates that we agree to it and welcome it. Because there are many societies in our region of space, they tend to hold each other in check and will take legal action against one another should the rules of conduct be violated.

7) There are other parts of the universe where great empires exist with their own rules and few competitors. Many nations have also joined together in associations of economic, political, and military, or all three for mutual trade and defense. These are quite common. The region where we live contains about 5,000 stars. This is a small part of the galaxy with important rules of conduct. There are also small empires here, both dictatorial and democratic.

8) Main thoroughfares are ruled by councils for safety and security. The councils exist in order to provide insurance against violence that could erupt and grow into war. Disputes occur frequently and are handled by negotiations or through legal procedures. In our region of space, societies are not allowed to have military forces, only security forces for their own defense.

9) True democracy does exist in the universe, but it is very rare. They must be very strong in their dealings with other societies in space. There is no one empire that is predominant because there is too much diversity of life here. There are many marvelous and wondrous creations and there are many societies that have achieved a very high state of awareness. But, they remain in the minority.

10) Collectives are different from Empires in that they have no source home planet. They have a group of planets that are dissimilar. They have joined together,

usually through conquest and persuasion, and have become a formidable force. Empires are usually centered in one world or region by one race. Collectives are made up of many races. Collectives may encompass hundreds of worlds and exist beyond vast reaches of space. They are always interested in gaining new allegiances and new members. They are highly organized and have a hierarchical structure.

11) Collectives are comprised of a series of races functioning at different levels of authority and command. The worker-class is bred to serve in specific functions. They have very little individuality or individual abilities of reasoning and discernment. They have a hive mentality and are rigidly controlled with no personal freedom. They are impressively efficient in very specific areas, but they have no insight and are not creative in their approaches. They rely on structure, codes of conduct, and their ability to manipulate the thoughts of others they influence.

12) Collectives are not military powers. They are economic powers. Their focus is on trade, resource acquisition, and building alliances. There are many Collectives functioning in our region. Other nations have established defenses against Collective's intervention in their trade, commerce, and internal affairs. Collectives must abide by rules of conduct or face grave consequences. They must use negotiations, diplomacy, and influence.

13) Collectives do not have an artistic appreciation of Earth. They need our resources and view Earth as a prize, the best among many. Nuclear weapons triggered their intervention on this planet. They realized that if we became strong and had greater technological power, their intervention here would become more difficult to achieve. They believe that they cannot wait. They seek to have humanity believe that they will save us from our own destruction.

14) Because they are prevented from having a military presence, they must take a long time and be very subtle in their influence with humanity. They want our help because they cannot breathe our air and take our resources themselves. They want to add humanity to their collective community and mentality. They want us to become a part of them. This adds to their strength and minimizes resistance.

15) This is why there is such an investment in time and energy in gaining our allegiance, in bonding with humanity through interbreeding, and in establishing a deep and pervasive association. In order to gain control over us, they must have us welcome them, want what they have to offer, seek their assistance, and believe that we need their help in order to satisfy the restraints that are placed upon them, according to the rules that have been established.

16) Sources for non-human entities originate in different sectors of space, both on and inside planets and planetoids or moons and in different harmonic frequency bands and dimensions that are outside the perceptive range of humans

as well as outside linear matter, energy, space and time. There are over 70 extra-terrestrial species interacting with this planet at this time. There are 9 that are the most active. They can be classified into three general categories of: (1) Human Looking, (2) Smooth Skinned Humanoids, and (3) Scaly Rough Skinned Reptilians.

The Nordics seem to have been pressing their nuclear nonproliferation concepts since the early 1950s, when they asked for a halt to what they saw as aggressive, warlike activities.

HUMAN LOOKING

1) This section covers all aspects of human looking extraterrestrials. This includes inter-dimensional entities, the Blond species, and aliens masquerading as humans. Although human-looking extraterrestrials generally appear to be benevolent towards humanity, there are many that have been influenced, controlled, or possessed by malevolent beings.

2) Any apparent alien who is essentially human and Caucasian in appearance, even though sometimes very tall, may be called a Blond. Though many are tall, blond-haired, and blue-eyed, certainly all are not. Even some of the American Indian connection may be considered Blond in origin. There are many factions of these aliens, from different places, with different motivations.

ANDROMEDIANS

1) There is a great force of entities coming from the Andromeda Galaxy. These are inter-stellar entities that go in light. Their craft have the ability to go in hyper-light so that, in only a matter of moments, they can be here from an entirely different star system.

2) These entities are very beautiful. They are lithely built and very thin. This race is so spiritually evolved that they no longer require a physical body. They are almost beings of light energy. They are illuminated in light. They are very tall and stand eight to ten feet in height. In mythology, they were referred to as the Winged Gods.

3) Their biological system is based entirely different than our genetic system. These entities display an embodiment that is magnetized in light. They do not eat. They gain knowledge. They live off of "Prona" which is an ancient term meaning truth.

4) They are beautiful beyond description and mankind shadows fragments of that beauty. They have taken care of humanity because they consider us as

their brothers and sisters. They believe that we all came from the same source and that we were all created in light. It is the common bond between us.

5) They have a very great Mother Ship. At night, it is invisible because of the metal that it is made out of. It looks black. But, if it were to light up, it would be the sun illuminated 10,000 times. It is here in our stratosphere. It moves quietly and stealthily. Our government is aware of its presence and it is ominous to them.

6) This ship is called Miria Amour. It means the silver light. The ship has warriors that would defy imagination. It can blast a continent to the bottom of the sea. It could rotate our planet and send it spinning out of orbit. The ship is here because of the disease on this planet. It is here because of the collapse of consciousness of civilization. It is here also because of the changes that are going to occur here. And, it is here because of another force that is engaged on this planet.

7) These beings have inspired profits, in the past, to do wonderful things and preserve the seeds of humanity. Its truth and its words have been misused, misconstrued, and taken by powerful men to enslave people. And, it has been allowed. But, these entities are back now for truth.

PLEIADIANS

1) The Pleiadians come from a small cluster of stars called the Pleiades. Of the seven stars, which make up the Pleiades cluster in the Taurus Constellation, the Pleiadians come from the star known as Taygeta. There are nine planets that revolve around Taygeta. Four of these planets are inhabited.

2) The Pleiadian's home world is the planet Erra, which is very similar to Earth, being only ten percent smaller. Nature there is also very similar, especially since samples of plants, minerals, and animals have been taken to the Pleiades and developed there. The surface gravity is slightly less than on Earth. A day on Erra is six tenths of a second less than on Earth.

3) The Pleiadians are humans with few physical differences. Their skin is whiter than humans as a result of higher evolution. They are several million years older than humanity. The Pleiadians live a more spiritual life style. This means that they are experiencing and learning more with their spiritual senses than with their material senses. There are no medical problems. They are able to control their health through psychic balance. The life span for a Pleiadian is more than 700 years. The ability to project thoughts to another place on the planet is very common and is the socially accepted method of visiting.

4) Only 400 million people live on Erra. Population control has come about in a desire to keep their society spread out and able to share the resources of the planet equally. Pleiadians on Erra live in a utopian world free of pollution, war, hunger, and disease thanks to advanced technology and spiritual awareness.

5) Because the population communicates by telepathy, there is no dishonesty. All basic necessities are provided freely, and anything beyond that is acquired through individual barter. There is no money and, hence, no irrational grasping for wealth and power. The Pleiadians have no economics, but do have a system of sharing the resources of their world. Material possessions are all provided, based on their contribution to the community.

6) There are no large cities with towering buildings as on Earth. But instead, the small population of Erra is spread out into smaller communities that span the planet, connected by a series of sentient tubeways that not only transport the population but educate and inform them along the way. The people live in more rural settings and keep a distance from each other.

7) Nearly all of the manufacturing and production of products for living is done on other planets in their solar system so as to not upset the ecology on Erra. They have long since developed a balance with nature that is well protected. The planet has a green atmosphere, which is controlled, and it contributes to their health and stress-less way of life.

8) What government is necessary is provided by a 'High Council' composed of the wisest and most evolved Pleiadians. Any changes to their social order must be approved by a vote of the highest percentage of the population. The Pleiadians are part of a federation of civilized worlds that live by the words of an advanced race in the Andromeda Galaxy.

9) It is the desire of Pleiadians to stimulate the human consciousness through the dissemination of information so that humanity can make the necessary changes to create a new world based on Saalome, which is a Pleiadian word meaning 'peace in wisdom'.

PROCYONIANS

1) Procyonians have been nick-named 'Swedes' and are on the average between six and six and a half feet tall. They are from a solar system that revolves

around Procyon, a binary yellow-white and yellow star system that rises before Sirius in Canis Minor (in the body of the Lesser Dog), about 11.4 light years from Earth. They are from the fourth planet in orbit around the Procyon double star system.

2) These Blonds are muscular with slender necks and agile bodies. Their eyes are alert and of high intelligence. Physically they are almost identical to humans. The main difference is that by human standards their blood circulatory system is under-developed, while their lymphatic system is over-developed. This gives them stronger immune systems than terrestrial humans.

3) Some Blonds have high intellectual and verbal abilities, while others are mute and telepathic. The Blonds with speech abilities will respond violently if attacked or threatened. But, the telepathic type will not. Both types are careful to avoid exposure, and usually encounter humans in quiet isolated places. They contact females more frequently. They may just stare and observe humans, then retreat. The Blonds do not seem to age, and consistently appear to be from 27 to 35 human years old, no matter what their real age may be.

4) Sometimes Blonds are prisoners of the Grays. The Grays must paralyze or destroy their ability to teleport through time and other dimensions in order to take them prisoner. The Blonds that are seen on the same ships as the Grays, working with them, are hybrids or they are clones. One way to distinguish the clone is that they all look alike. The real Blonds have distinct facial feature differences, and do not look alike.

5) The clones have thick necks and coarsely muscular bodies. They do not have the ability to teleport or to travel inter-dimensionally. They can be contacted by telepathy, but are unable to send. They can be given orders telepathically. They are zombie-like flesh robots. You can tell that they are of low intelligence by looking into their eyes.

6) The tall Blonds from Procyon have a benign attitude toward humanity, except for their strong disapproval of our inhumanity to each other. This strong disapproval is further intensified by the fact that our government has made a secret alliance with their hereditary enemies, the Grays, in order to obtain even more destructive weapon systems than those that were already in existence. Our government is not interested in negotiating with the Procyonians, as they would not provide us with weapon systems.

ALIENS MASQUERADING AS HUMANS

1) The purpose of aliens who masquerade as humans are so that they may perform certain activities on Earth without suspicion. These activities include the study of human development, the transfer of information to humanity, and the direct intervention and control of human activities for alien purposes. Aliens who have been acting in this manner include the following:

* Pleiadeans – for benevolent study and spiritual development.

* Nordics – the Nordic/Aryan race forefathers.

* Koldasians – similar level of evolution.

* Ashtarians – for the advancement of religious dogma.

* Gray controlled bio-drones, droids – to replace Earth's leaders for social and economic control.

* Gray controlled Men In Black, holograms, and projections – for mystical figures that appear to give divine guidance.

2.1.2 Smooth Skinned Humanoids

1) Smooth skinned humanoids, presented in this section, include: the Tall Grays, the Short Grays, Human/Grey Interbreeds, Zeta Reticulans, Sirians, Insectoids, and others. These are all humanoid beings with a body that has a head, two arms, and two legs similar to the human body. However, these beings have a physiology that is obviously not human in nature.

TALL GRAYS

1) Some of the various 22 sub-species of Grays originally started out as tall blond-haired humanoids in the Rigel system, but were subject to heavy radiation due to a nuclear exchange over a long period of time, changing their DNA to the point where some of the species became stunted misshapen dwarves. Glandular structures were also affected, including reproductive and digestive organs. The nuclear exchange occurred approximately 300,000 years ago. This type of Gray species has been referred to as the "Orion Crusaders" or the "Markabians".

2) There are two main types of the tall Gray species who call themselves the EBAN. Type 1 of the Orion Grays are about seven to eight feet tall and have what you would call an insect-base to their genetic makeup. They have a pronounced nose and slanted black eyes. They have no external genitalia and are extremely aggressive toward humans. Type 2 of the tall Grays, are between six and seven feet tall and have external genitalia. This type appears to be a taller form of the short Gray species with similar large heads and large black eyes.

3) The Grays operate very efficiently in the dark. Their eyes are more sensitive to ultraviolet light. They have the ability to control their heart rate. The normal heart rate for a Gray is above that of a human. The skin seems to have a metallic content and an unusual, cobalt pigmentation.

4) The brain has been described as having many more lobes than the human brain. There have been previous references to crystalline networks that have been found in the brains of some of the alien autopsies. It is believed that the network has a functional relationship to telepathic communication and acts as a functional node for group control of the cloned species, which function in what is essentially a hive mind.

5) They have problems with their glands, particularly with their sebaceous glands, which make it difficult for them to digest food. They derive nourishment from the glandular secretions and enzymes that they extract from animals that they mutilate. They absorb these extracts through the pores in their skin.

6) The Gray species is not based on individualization or being an individual entity. For entities maintaining a group mind set (social memory complex), individualization seems to cause a great deal of random energy loss. They were initially fascinated with both human individuality and the human emotional spectrum, which they can perceive but apparently do not comprehend what it means (to humans).

7) This species objectives appear to be founded on a rigid domination survival-based social order, where their "religion" is science, their social structure is geared to obedience, and their military concepts are grouped around conquest, colonization, and domination through covert mind control programs. It has become apparent that there are definite hierarchies within their social structures that provide for each entity having specific duties to perform.

8) These beings have technological superiority, but they appear to be lacking in spiritual and social sciences. This is evident in their obvious lack of warmth, emotionality, and respect relative to humans. They can sometimes obtain momentary pleasure in terms of mood elevation by tuning in on human wavelengths via telepathically connected radionic devices. They react to intense human emotion such as ecstasy or agony. They blanket couples for sexual thrills and are drawn to aberrants and sexual deviates. The Markabs use sex, pain, drugs and fear as obsessive elements with which to aberrate humans.

9) There appears to be much subtle conditioning that has helped prepare Earth people for certain aliens. However, it is now clear the aliens that have made technology available to the secret government are not benevolent but are our enemies, as they do the abductions, lie, deceive, are generally malevolent and are apparently implementing a very carefully planned covert invasion which includes the brutal and inhumane use of humans and animals for advanced genetic experimentation and crossbreeding.

10) It is a strategy whereby the malevolent aliens are building an 'Faustian' alliance with the secret government to enable them to effectively claim the Earth for their own, with humanity's unwitting consent, before any other aliens are able to effect appropriate contact within the constraints of so called 'Universal Laws' to which other alien races supposedly adhere.

11) The malevolent aliens have claimed their total authorship of the religions as a means to inculcate humanity's dependence and prospective allegiance to them and reverence of them. Their apparent behavior indicates an attempt to leverage that claimed authorship to their own benefit by placing themselves in

the position of being 'Gods' or 'God's divine messengers'.

SHORT GRAYS

1) The large Grays use smaller cloned, big-headed Grays to perform abduction and examination work. It is these Grays that abductees see most of the time. They are referred to as the Belletrax species from Betelgeuse in the Orion Constellation.

2) The Gray species in general is more on the order of an electronically based space society with a common social memory complex that allows them to collectively function as areas of group-mind. Groups of Grays are controlled from one central source being, usually one of the large Grays, a Blond humanoid, or other dominant species.

3) The approximate height of the big-headed Gray is 3.5 to 4.5 feet tall, and have an average weight of about 40 pounds. Proportions of the head to the body are similar to a human five-month fetus. This seems to reflect a very ancient nature as a species as well as the fact that their DNA patterns lie within a specific band that is on a more primitive scale.

4) The species skin tone variation seems to be widespread, with skin colors ranging from bluish gray to beige, tan, brown, or white. There are factors that affect skin color, and one of them is the state of general health of the entity. Skin color is known to change after they have consumed nourishment.

5) There are no reproductive organs or reproductive capability with the cloned species. The brain capacity is estimated to be between 2500 and 3500 cc, compared to 1300 cc of humans. Due to the cloning process, the neural matter is artificially grown brain matter. The Grays have technology that enables them to insert memory patterns and consciousness into clones in any manner or pattern that they wish.

6) They have two separate brains with many more lobes than human brains, and contain a crystalline network for telepathic communication and group control. The cloned species function in essentially a hive mind. Their movement is deliberate, slow, and precise.

7) The Grays consume nourishment through a process of absorption through their skin. The process, according to abductees who have witnessed it, involves spreading a biological slurry mixture that has been mixed with hydrogen peroxide (which oxygenates the slurry and eliminates bacteria) onto their skin. Waist products are then excreted back through the skin. Many abductees have noticed that the Grays have a distinct series of odors, many of them appear to be similar to a mentholated cinnamon smell.

8) The Gray clones have one major organ that has the combined function of a heart and lung. The rest of their body consists of a homogeneous spongy tissue infused with circulatory systems, glands, and other amorphous structures. Each

of the Gray clones has an individuality, but it is much less pronounced than in the human, where tendencies toward expanded awareness and shared consciousness are minimized through cultural conditioning, programming, and basic cranial differences in structure.

9) The clones are subservient to the taller Grays. The smaller Grays possess an electronically monitored and controlled social memory complex that allows them to function effectively in a group-mind mode. They do not have distinct individuality, as the larger Grays have. When one of the Grays dies, its implant serves as a focusing device for retrieval of the body. When Grays die, their bodies are "beamed" away.

HUMAN/GRAY INTERBREEDS

1) The Grays are cross-breeding with human beings in an attempt to populate the Earth with hybrid beings that serve their agenda for global domination. This activity has been going on for a long time and has produced many generations of Crossbreeds. These crossbreeds are potentially more superior in function than either humans or Grays.

2) Many individuals have seen breeding labs, both underground and on spacecraft. In those labs, Gray fetuses can be seen. Those fetuses have heads that are "out of proportion" to their body as compared to humans.

3) The Gray clones are abducting human females, both temporarily and permanently, and using them for cross-breeding in order to produce a new hybrid species that does not serve humanity.

4) The Grays do understand the concept of bonding, but only intellectually in terms of bonding (between a human mother/ ovum source and an alien cross-bred child) that will serve to contribute to the survival of the cross-breed. They recognize the need for it in the child only in terms of survival.

5) Thousands of years ago, many races interbred here to create an intelligent and adaptive being. But, the current interbreeding is to create humans that will serve the Visitors. Interbreeding enables

them to establish a presence and commanding influence here. Interbreeding has been going on for several generations. It is becoming very successful.

6) There are hybrids that are living among us in our world today. There are not many, but there will be ever more in the future. These are intelligent humans that do not serve humanity. There are also hybrids that actually possess the Visitor's consciousness. Soon, the Visitors will be able to live on the surface of our planet permanently.

ZETA RETICULANS

1) The Zeta Reticuli Grays have an insect-based genetic system and are about 3.5 to 4.5 feet in height. They have no external genitalia. They are less aggressive toward humans than the other Gray species. These beings are from Zeta Reticuli in the Reticulum Constellation. These humanoids have very distinctive facial features with a turned-up nose and long slender neck.

2) The Reticulans appear to be a highly aware grouping of entities that function as a social memory complex. Individuality appears to exist, but is overshadowed by the group mind. The Reticulans are millions of years old as a species and have a weakened DNA structure as the result of conflicts that involved nuclear radiation. The Reticulans have relied on artificial reproduction or cloning and face extinction from incurable diseases. They are creating hybrid human-Reticulans capable of mating with humans.

3) The Reticulans are largely involved in scientific exobiological surveys as well as systemic geological observation and field studies. Their civilization appears to be totally dedicated to interstellar research and life analysis. The Network has been on Earth for the past 50 years.

4) The basic objectives of the Reticulans is to use nullification and domination to control the leaders of various targeted civiliza-

A Zeta alien, looking smug and cocky.

tions. They accomplish this by taking out the leaders and replacing them with entities they can control.

5) Military operations of the Reticulan species consist of colonization of unprotected civilizations for the purpose of setting up logistical supply depots, slave sources, acquisition of potential allies, and biological materials.

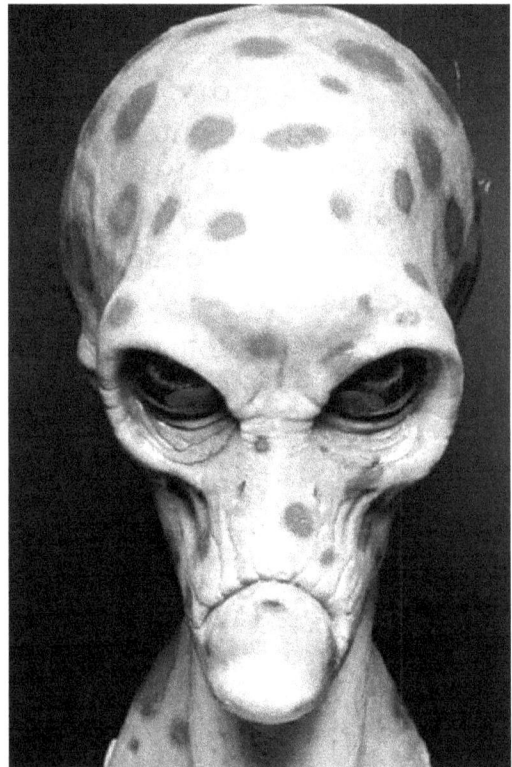

6) The process of conquering a planet involves location of beings that vibrate in resonance with their vibrational frequency. These located beings are then told that they are the Elite or Chosen Ones who will conquer or lead the human race and rule the world for their Gray masters.

7) Often the located beings are physically taken aboard a craft and given physical examinations, provided with implants, given accelerated data through inculcation methods that will help them serve the Grays. The function of the Elite is to decimate portions of its own race in an effort to reduce populations to manageable limits so the remainder can be easily controlled.

SIRIANS

1) Sirius apparently possesses qualities that develop some highly unusual personalities. Known as the Dog Star, in the constellation Canis Major, it is the brightest star in the firmament, and more than twenty times as luminous as our own sun.

2) The Sirians are a hybrid race with traits that are similar to the Blonds and Reptilian species. They are similar in appearance to humans except for the eyes, which have vertical slit pupils, and an elongated nose. They have short blond body hair under the tight fitting body suit uniforms that they wear.

3) The Sirians are actively involved in a war with the Grays from the Orion constellation. They have formed an alliance with the tall Blonds against the Grays. They are working in underground bases on Earth for the purposes of abducting humans and programming them. They are also performing genetic work there with humanoid forms.

4) Sirian Females have long hair, feminine features, and breasts. One female has been seen wearing a blue two-piece uniform with a pendant on her forehead. The males wear tight fitting hoods with round-shaped radio receivers and short antenna over their left ears. The insignia over their left breast is triangular in shape with either three parallel lines across it or a winged serpent inside of it.

INSECTOIDS

1) Although there appears to be a large variety of extraterrestrials in the form of insects, the most common and advanced species appears to be a giant insect creature, two meters (6'6) tall that resembles a Praying Mantis. It should be noted that experiencers feel that this type is no insect, but rather an intelligent, gentle-spirited, but somewhat "hyper" and jerky-moving, human-like lifeform, both males and females.

2) These Beings have long, narrow faces, with long, narrow, large eyes, sharply slanted upward and outward in an almost narrow-V position, given an almost insect-like appearance. This comparison is heightened by the Praying-Mantis types' extremely thin, long torsos, long, extremely-thin arms which are usually crooked into a sharp bend at the mid-joint, with the hand and fingers/

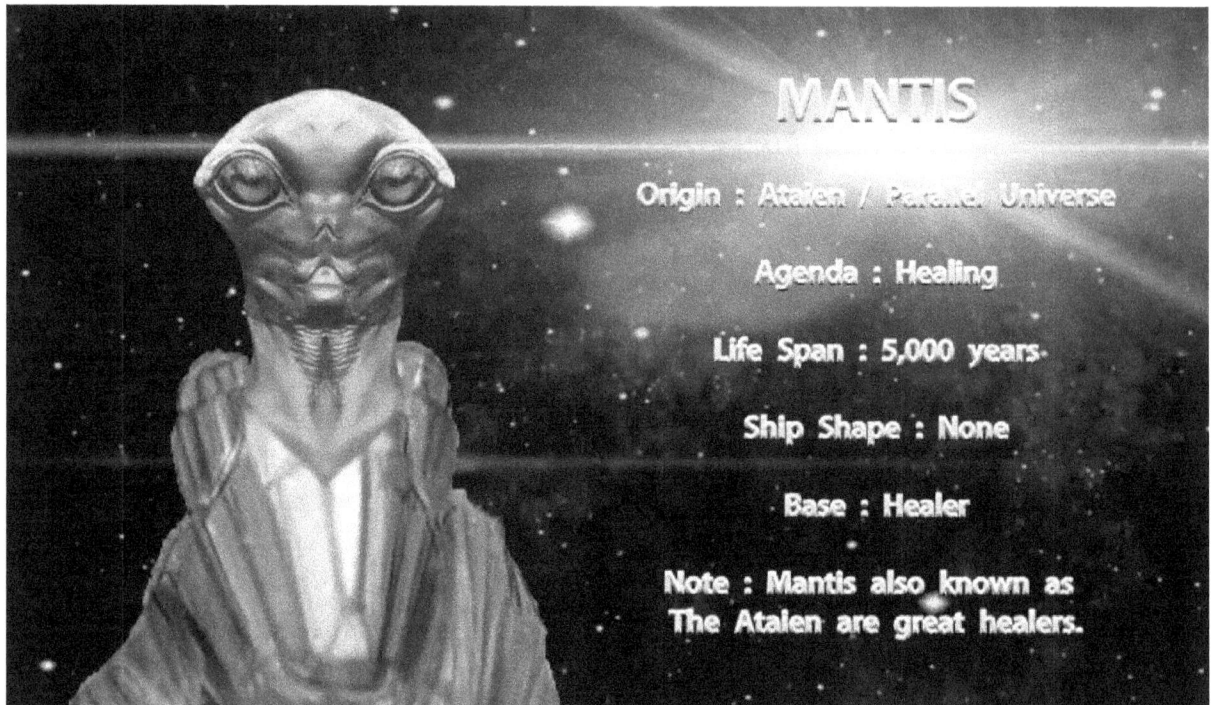

MANTIS

Origin : Ataien / Parallel Universe

Agenda : Healing

Life Span : 5,000 years

Ship Shape : None

Base : Healer

Note : Mantis also known as The Ataien are great healers.

Evidence indicates they are taking away - abducting - humans, a good percentage of them young women.

mitten sloping almost vertically downward from the "wrist", and legs also bent at an almost right-angle at the mid-joint, creating a crouched pose. The overall effect is the characteristic "Praying Mantis" look.

3) Witnesses have reported seeing this strange and frightening being on several occasions. In Maryland, in 1973, a group of four Praying Mantis aliens abducted a law student and examined him. On another occasion, a creature, fitting the same description, was found attacking a teenage boy.

The boy was rescued with some difficulty and the being was chased away.

OTHER SMOOTH SKINNED HUMANOIDS

1) Other species of this type include the Akartians, Iargans, Dwarfs, Hairies (Yeti type, Sasquatch), and Ummo's. Another group is from the Arcturus system. These humanoids have red hair and have been called Oranges. They remain neutral toward humans and are waiting to reclaim a portion of the Earth for themselves.

2) Another group of entities that have a more pessimistic view of human fitness for being in charge of the planet's resources is a very large humanoid race that are described in the book of Genesis as the Nephilim (literally giants) who impregnated human females who then gave birth to giants. This race is reported to originate from the constellation of Lyra and inhabits the planet Nibiru.

3) There is an on-world presence of humanoid races that have historically assisted humanity in its evolutionary development. Such a race has been the remnants of the ancient Lemurian and Atlantean civilizations that established large

crystalline cities inside the Earth's crust after abandoning their cities/civilizations established on the Earth's surface. They are a tall Nordic-looking race living in a subterranean city under the North Pole. Strictly speaking, this group is not extraterrestrial in origin but simply a sub-terrestrial humanoid race that is genetically linked to humanity.

4) Another group of extraterrestrials are off-world ETs that intervene to assist humanity in dealing with off-world ET races. This category is commonly described as 'Nordics' and 'Semites' that come from Altair Alpha Centauri, who are humanoid in appearance, between 7-8 feet in height. Altair's fourth and fifth planets are inhabited. In fact, the people from Altair colonized the Pleiades system long ago. The human-looking Pleiadean extraterrestrials are actually ancestrally Altairians. There are two variants, the Semitic-looking ones and the Nordic-looking ones.

SCALY ROUGH SKINNED REPTILIANS

1) Scaly rough skinned humanoids describe the appearance of the Reptilian species from the Draco constellation and the Capella System. These beings have elongated heads and eyes with vertical slit pupils. Some of the reptilian hierarchy are albino white and not the usual green or brown. Some have conical horns midway between the brow and the top of the skull.

2) For the most part, we are dealing with another species that is humanoid in shape, but Reptilian in heritage. Their leader elite are the "Draco" that have special "wings", which are flaps of skin, supported by long ribs. These can be folded back against the body. They are also known as the "Dragon Race" and their symbology usually includes a Winged Serpent. There are elements of their species that do not have wings – the "soldier class" and "scientists" have none.

3) They are all 'cold blooded' and must have a balanced environment to maintain body temperature. The "soldier class" of the species can bury themselves in the ground and wait long periods of time in order to ambush their enemy. If need be they can survive on one very large meal every few weeks or even once a year. As a species, they are well suited for space travel due to their ability to hibernate. These reptoids have scales that protect them from moisture loss. They have no sweat glands.

4) The scales (scutes) are much larger on their backs, making the skin waterproof. The scales elsewhere on the body are more flexible. They have three fingers with an opposing thumb. The eyes are catlike and large. They have twin nostrils at the end of a short stubby muzzle. They are mostly meat eaters. The mouth is more like a slit, but they do have teeth that are differentiated into incisors, canines, and molars. They average from 6 to 7 feet in height.

5) The Reptilian (amphibian) humanoids have been interacting with Earth for ages. Many contactees and abductees repeatedly describe an insignia of a

Flying Serpent on the shoulder patch, badge, medallion or helmet. The Serpent Race lives under the ground.

6) The Draconian Group is a Confederation with subgroups (The "Serpent Race" from Sirius) and various crossbreeds. They set up bases inside of Venus, the Earth, and other locations. Earth is on their ancient space trade routes.

7) The Draco are about 8 feet tall and have winged appendages coming out of their shoulders, dark scaly skin, and have glowing red eyes. They have the ability to fly and usually operate at night. These entities, as well as the elite of the other Reptilian species (that also have winged appendages) were the source for some of the legends of the past relating to Gargoyles and Valkyries. It is also apparent that some of the qualities ascribed to vampires have also been taken from these creatures.

8) Some Reptilians eat humans like we eat chicken. In the United States, there are great, underground food-storage rooms full of preserved human bodies. Sometimes the bodies are those of children. It is not only children but also adults that Reptilians eat. However, children are preferred because they are not poisoned with substances like caffeine, nicotine, alcohol and other things that adults are saturated with.

9) The Reptilians don't seem to be dependent on humans as a food source, although part of their experimental work with us is toward the end of future food supply/production. When they become involved with crossbreeding (humans and Reptilians), they are not doing it for racial survival but for the purpose of creating a subclass (slave race) within their own culture. These half-breeds are to be biological war machines and laborers, etc. They are to be someone else's property.

10) The Reptilians seem to have little regard for us as living beings. (They think we are as ugly and repulsive to them as we ever portrayed them to be, and that we, the human race, are "as valuable as weeds".) However, they do seem to consider some of us valuable property. One gets the feeling they will continue to use us as they see fit, or, if we ever become a real problem as a group, they would sooner wipe us out than deal with us.

11) They do not fear humanity and consider themselves far superior to humans by all comparisons. They supposedly consider the surface of this planet to be a poisonous, inhospitable environment and "allow" us to live here, since they live below the surface and in space. (We and our surface environment function as a physical buffer or living shield around their home underground.)

A SHOCKING LOOK INSIDE THE
'GOVERNMENT-ALIEN EXCHANGE PROGRAM'
Timothy Green Beckley

In the Spring of 1989, UFO UNIVERSE, edited by Tim Beckley, published an article by Robert W. Boyajian, titled *'CONQUEST EARTH? - A SHOCKING LOOK INSIDE THE GOVERNMENT-ALIEN EXCHANGE PROGRAM,'* which included an exclusive interview with Sergeant Clifford Stone, on assignment at Roswell, New Mexico.

For the most part the article dealt with an ongoing treaty between the U.S. and at least one group of ultra terrestrials.

The following consists of a direct pick up of the material as originally printed to a limited audience.

"In the course of my UFO investigations, I established contact with Aileen Edwards, Director of the UFO Contact Center International,Seattle, Washington. For several years, Aileen has been doing excellent work getting people released from mental institutions that do not understand the UFO contact or abduction phenomenon. Many of these unfortunate patients have been given dangerous neurolytic drugs as means of 'treating' their 'illness.'

"As a result of our conversations, Aileen placed me in touch with Sergeant Clifford Earl Stone of the United States Army, who is currently stationed at Roswell, New Mexico, which is near the site of the most famous crash-UFO case of all time which allegedly took place in 1947, and involved the recovery of several alien bodies by the military.

"What I have found out by speaking with Sergeant Stone can only be labeled 'sensational.' But before we get to the main body of our interview, I should point out that much of his testimony can now be verified by others connected with the intelligence community. For example, recently there was aired on national television a two hour special, *'UFO COVERUP - LIVE FROM WASHINGTON.'*

AMERICA'S TOP SECRET TREATY WITH ALIEN LIFE FORMS

Among the most interesting features of this program were the on-the-air confessions of two mysterious individuals whose true identities remain a secret, but who go by the code names 'Falcon' and 'Condor.' Their faces were hidden at all times, and their voices altered through a muting device.

"From what I have discovered, however, Falcon is an OSI agent, while Condor is a scientist working for the U.S. government.

"On the show, Condor told of a deal the government made with the aliens: 'Essentially, the agreement says that we won't disclose your existence if you won't interfere in our society, and we allow you to operate from a designated base in the United States.' It's in the state of Nevada, in an area called Area 51. Extraterrestrials have complete control of the base.

"My understanding is that three different aliens of the same species has resided in the U.S. from 1948 or 1949 until the present day. The first alien was captured inthe New Mexican desert after its craft crashed. The alien, which was named EBE by the government was kept in captivity for three years and we learned a great deal of information about the alien's race, culture and spacecraft. The second alien was part of an exchange program. The third alien was also part of an exchange program and has been the guest of the U.S. government since 1982.

"This knowledge has long been classified at exceedingly high levels, and has not been released even though various court battles have been fought to obtain the truth under the Freedom of Information Act. The much talked-about MJ-12 briefing document was a 'leak' made by sources unknown, there have been several others, and yet further revelations have been promised by those working inside the 'establishment' who are convinced the public must be told EVERYTHING and NOW!..."

The interview between Mr. Boyajion of UFO UNIVERSE and Sgt. Stone went as follows:

UFO UNIVERSE: *In reference to Condor's statement about Area 51 in the state of Nevada, what do you personally feel about this in your studies?*

CLIFFORD STONE: I believe that the American people has a right to know what is going on...

UU: *Do you feel there's a war going on perhaps between different types of aliens?*

CS: Yes, I do. I believe what is presently termed the 'greys' may very well be the (entities) that the U.S. government has the pact with right now, and they are not necessarily the 'good guys.'

UU: *Do you feel that these grey guys are evil?*

CS: Well...there are some things I prefer not to talk about. But I'll tell you this much. First, I believe that there is a God. And I firmly believe that God made man and all intelligent life to be a free agent, to chose HIS own validity. Abductions are REAL. Abductions are taking place. People are being forced to undergo - partake in various experiments - for whatever reason by our alien visitors.

UU: *What else would give you the impression that these guys are evil, cut and dry? Is there a case you can cite?*

CS: O.K., this is supposition. One gentleman who was doing research into it reported a military intrusion on an alien base, right here in New Mexico. Well, the military tried to go in and take over the base (It was mentioned that a similar event took place in Nevada). Sixty-six servicemen were supposedly killed there. The aliens had the base, it was an underground base and allegedly the military sent in some of their elite forces, probably equated to a Delta force, elite, anti-terrorist force, if you wish.

UU: *How did they find this base?*

CS: Well, it was part of the allegedly secret agreement that we would let them have bases, therefore we knew about the base. There was some type of argument that broke out between our people and the aliens.

UU: *So there are many bases throughout the country?*

CS: There are rumors of many bases. Given that these stories are true, I think that they probably have 12 or fewer bases. The greys may have various, let's say, hideouts. As far as actual full scale operational bases, there's probably 12 or fewer.

UU: *And where are you getting your information?*

CS: From, we'll say, other researchers that wish to remain sort of silent.

UU: *What position are you in the army at present?*

CS: I'm in an ROTC assignment.

UU: *How long have you been in the army?*

CS: Twenty years.

UU: *Your friends who remain anonymous are within the different services of the government I take it?*

CS: Well, for example, I was stationed at an Air Force base and one guy went and came to my home and identified himself as a fighter pilot and told me about an aircraft that he was piloting. I believe it was over the Pacific Ocean. Anyhow, it got real dark all of a sudden. He reported looking up and he and the other crew members saw what they described as a vehicle that was 3 miles long (Three miles in a circular expansion). As far as I know it stayed with them for 15 or 20 minutes and then went straight over the aircraft and got out in front of them and shot straight up, out of sight.

UU: *Where did you derive the idea that our government is making deals with aliens? What gave you this type of notion?*

CS: The Snowbird document. This document refers to us making primitive contact with the aliens in 1959. On April 25, 1964, we managed to carry on a 3 hour conversation which was the onset of the agreement at a base here in New Mexico. I believe that base was Holloman Air Force Base. The agreement involving an exchange oftechnology and our silence. By going ahead and not having any interference with the aliens, in exchange they gave us the technology and we agreed to keep quiet about their presence. That right there is sinister in itself.

UU: *How do you mean sinister in itself?*

CS: We have to go back to the abductions. For some reason they don't want the people to remember what happened. Well here you have people who had contact with alien beings, who have lost everything. They've went ahead and have family problems, they've lost their jobs, a lot of them have become reclusive, they have mental problems because they can't cope with what happened to them. They know that they've had some type of experience, but a lot of the time they would have nightmares. They can't explain these.

UU: *Because it was repressed in their subconscious?*

CS: Correct. Maybe by design, or it may be just because the body's own self-defensive mechanism is trying to cope with something that is beyond it's comprehension...

UU: *What about the benevolent beings that are said to exist, who abide by higher laws that do not allow them to interfere - aren't they trying to help?*

CS: The good guys are, well, I like to refer to them as being nomadic. What you're talking about, about the non-intervention with other intelligent life forms is a universal law. The nomadics go along with that. The greys violated the universal law.

UU: *What else can you say about the benevolent space beings?*

CS: They have a high regard for life. I believe, shall we say, 'the good forces,' they don't really want any interaction with us. They choose to just go ahead and just observe.

UU: *Silent guardians. So it seems what they're trying to do is balance what the greys imbalanced.*

CS: I would agree with that...

UU: *When you were describing that there are approximately 3 different types of hostile aliens from Zeta Reticuli, would you describe further what you mean by that?*

CS: At present time, I believe that the government has identified several groups. We break these down by EBE (extraterrestrial biological entities) type 1,2,3 - I think we are about up to 7 that have been identified (however, as Lear and others indicate, these seem to fall into either the reptilian or human categories - Branton). Well...seven types of space travelers, or inter-dimensional travelers, if you wish. When I refer to inter- dimensional travel, I am referring, utilizing the Einsteinian, Rosen, Bridges for that travel... I'm going to tell you the situation as I understand now. The greys will eventually come forth and try to state that they created Christ. This is not the case. They did not create Christ. Christ was and is a divine entity. He was sent here by the Creator, not the Creator of just the world, but the universe. I believe that they (the greys) are involved with the actual cattle mutilations. Now there are some copycats, and the government tries to get mileage off the copycats, and the government may have even went ahead and staged some - just to throw off the extraterrestrial connection.

UU: *Can you give more detail... regarding the greys, the subtleties ahead, and how to avoid any mishap?*

CS: You mean how to identify if your working with a good guy or bad guy? For one thing there are the religious (activities) the bad guys are not happy with. For example, there was an instance where they tried to pick up a farmer...he started to pray and they couldn't take him aboard the craft... He kept praying and finally they gave up trying to abduct him. There was also an incident in Vietnam where a UFO set down in a field. It terrorized some of the villagers, and there was a soldier who was out visiting his girlfriend, who would later become his wife. Anyhow, he got tied up there and the UFO was trying to convince some of the people they should go. It wanted to take some of the people. The soldier stood his ground and wouldn't let the entities do it. The M16 that the soldier had was impervious to the aliens, but the cross that he always wore, and he always carried a Bible, they had regard for that. Finally, they gave up and decided not to try to take any of the people.

UU: *What type of mentality are we dealing with when we're talking about the secret deals made with ETs?*

CS: Let's go back and look at what happened as far as our deepening involvement at the onset of the Vietnam war. Take a look at what happened with the Iran affair. The situation is that there are elements within our government that sometimes act all on their own without congressional restraints, which ultimately affects the entire American population. In this case, it will ultimately have an affect on the entire population of the world. Up until about 1985, I would not have believed any of this. As a result of coming into contact with the SNOWBIRD DOCUMENT, I am left with no recourse but to believe that we have made these agreements - rightly or wrongly. I believe what is going to eventually happen is that they will make themselves known and immediately go ahead and try to destroy society as we know society...

UU: *On the broadcast 'UFO COVERUP LIVE', they spoke of an exchange program where we sent two of our guys up into their crafts. This aspect of the exchange program, do you feel any of this is true?*

CS: It follows accepted diplomatic procedures.

UU: *What is the purpose of revealing this information at this time?*

CS: I think it's to try to prepare the American public for the ultimate disclosure of the existence of the alien beings. I think there is the effort for the good guys to make contact with the people within our government, but I think now what is happening is that the U.S. government learned in 1983 or thereabout that they are NOT dealing with the good guys, but really don't know what to do about it.

UU: *So how can they get out of this? What would your suggestion be?*

CS: Well, my suggestion would be to stand up to the greys. Let them know that this is a free society, that we are not going to sit back and let anyone - be they from outer space or some other foreign country - convert the people of the United States.

UU: *You said that the government didn't know that they were dealing with the bad guys at first. How would the government figure out that these entities were evil? What would make them think that? What would make them decide all of a sudden?*

CS: Let us suppose that we make a deal with a group of aliens. Among other things we agreed that they can have prearranged bases. We will provide security and we will not acknowledge their existence to the general public. In return, they're going to go ahead and carry on certain experimentations, gathering various minerals, getting various flora, various animal life. They're also going to go ahead and conduct some experiments or some research on human beings. Now this troubles us because we don't want that to get out of hand, so we bargain a little deeper and we come to the agreement that, okay, if you abduct anyone we need to know who they are so that if there are any problems in the future we can go ahead and take care of those people who may need medical or psychological attention, so we can assist with this. They say, fine, we will provide you with say a list of all abductees. Later, we find out that they are providing us with maybe a hundred or two hundred abductions maybe every couple of months, but we discover that the number is really into the thousands. We also find out that this scientific curiosity is also being used to tag these people, i.e. the implants, and we are not being told why they are doing this. Now we no longer have control over the abductions. We might even find that there might even be a scarier aspect to it - let's say some of these abductees appear to be 'sleepers,' there is some type of information that they're being fed, a post-hypnotic suggestion for lack of a better term. But don't think that this is hypnotic at all - it's not. It is a very much advanced technological process. Anyhow, they are being told at a certain time, a certain place in the future, they are going to be required to recall things that they are being told at this time, right toward the end of the experimentation or whatever is going on. However, alien forces want this to be kept so secret that if you try to pull this out of them while they're under hypnosis, it will cause the body functions to become under stress.

UU: *Have there been any intervention with the benevolent beings in this matter?*

CS: I would say that we know of several—should we say—intergalactic fights that have taken place...dogfights.

UU: *An obvious dispute among aliens themselves? What do you feel was the outcome?*

CS: The good won. Right now I think that the good are trying to'build up their forces.' I think the greys were very concerned about the crash at Roswell, New Mexico, because we had something that they were identifying as a weapons system - and that was a very strong radar tracking system. They lost several ships to that. The aliens initially, having identified that as a weapons system of ours, adjusted their craft so that the high powered radar would not cause on-board difficulties. The greys assisted in keeping the story quiet about the Roswell incident without - how can I put this - 'open contact' with the government at that time (Note: This is conceivable as radar operates through powerful electromagnetic rays and thus may have an adverse affect on a craft utilizing electromagnetic propulsion or operational systems - Branton).

UU: *Have you heard of such a thing as MIB or Men In Black in relation to such incidents as these?*

CS: Yes. There is a well known newsperson who was involved with the UFO crash here in Roswell in 1947. He had his life threatened if he tried to go ahead and break the story. He's maintained silence ever since. He's talked a couple of times, but will never come out and fully tell the whole story.

UU: *Did any of the occupants make themselves known to our people at that time?*

"CS: Here again, I'd have to go back to the reporter who was approached by an entity. And I don't think the entity that he was approached by was of this Earth. It was your classic MIB saying, 'Look, stay out of this one!' Point blank he was told, 'If you try to break the story, you'll die. Around that time we also started to lose jet aircraft that were sent aloft to intercept UFOs. Most of the time these were written off as aircraft having malfunctioned that caused their crash. Some of the aircraft simply vanished without a trace. One incident happened here in Roswell, probably early 1950s. The family still lives here. Two aircraft were sent aloft to intercept a UFO and make the identification of the object as picked up on radar. One plane returned. To this day, one plane and a pilot never returned.

UU: *Is there any information in reference to the joint operations that such a government-alien alliance is doing beneath the Earth?*

CS: Supposition (is) there's a lot of genetic work going on down there. For example, there have been people who have claimed to have been taken to underground installations where they observed comatose people in these underground installations. There are also reports of various vats with human parts. One woman reported seeing what appeared as a very Earthly male who was in a vat of some type of fluid in one of the underground installations. Quite a few of the people have alleged that they have been taken to these underground installations and have been kept there for days.

UU: *And why were they let free once they knew of such an installation, let's say, if they're trying to hush that up?*

CS: The vast majority, the man on the street isn't going to believe them anyhow. There are allegations that some are either military or working with the government that were brought down there.

UU: *Are you saying that you are not very clear on what goes on down there? You've never met anyone who had anymore to say on it?*

CS: I'm saying I can't be very clear.

UU: *In other words, it's a little too intense to talk about?*

CS: Yes. I have an interest in UFOs and I've had to recently go through one heck of a battle with the military to express my first amendment right to voice my dissatisfaction with the U.S. government keeping this information suppressed. There are certain things that even as a private citizen that I have to be very careful about suggesting.

UU: *What part of the government would have jurisdiction in association with these aliens?*

CS: They would probably be the National Security Agency, they report directly to the National Security Council. As a matter of fact, it sets in on the National Security Council.

UU: *Are there people within this agency that realize that they've gotten into a little mess?*

CS: Yes, I think so. I think right now those that are in the know are sort of divided as to whether they should go public or try to keep it secret. The TV show **'UFO COVERUP'**, wasn't really well handled. They didn't really know how to go about bringing out the information that they do have. The situation is that of a programming process, the government wanted some of that information to be released. That I feel is a fact. Now they took that program from Washington and they really wanted to see what the reaction of the American society would be as a whole. How we would react to it. If the U.S. government ever comes forth and states - and eventually I feel within a very few short years, possibly even months - they're going to have to do that. They're going to have to come out and say that UFOs are a reality.

UU: *I heard you were going to Germany?*

CS: I will be separated from my family for at least two years as a result of it. They were going to put me out of the Army because of my interest in UFOs. I want to stay in right now - when I get out I want it to be my choice, not because they forced me out. Are you aware that this is a very, very hard subject matter? I mean it's so far out in left field I avoid it...but I'll bring it up anyhow. Do you know that there are reports that some of the alien ships do a harvest of the souls? In other words, they feed off the living energy, which is in fact the living soul.

UU: *Have you read Budd Hopkins' books?*

CS: Yes, I read both Budd Hopkins' books. Budd is very close to the truth, but the full truth is a horror story that is beyond any science fiction that you have ever read.

UU: *Are there entities of the more benevolent sort that are abducting people?*

CS: That's correct. What they do, I would say, that they have more of a sci-entific curiosity (referring her to the blondes? - Branton).

UU: *They have more of a compassion, you would say?*

CS: Correct. As a matter of fact, if there was a situation where you had a weapon that could kill them and they could not escape, other than do you harm, they would permit themselves to be killed. The situation with the abduction cases, in dealing with the bad guys, is that they will go ahead and make a person try to recall the bad times of their lives. Then the people relive those experiences, they go back to the way they felt when that experience was happening, they bring to mind the things they fear the most, they bring this out because they actually ab-sorb something similar to osmosis these feelings that they actually feed off of. . . feed off of our fear? - Branton)

UU: *So you're saying that these particular entities that are working in this fash-ion are the very entities that our government made these deals with?*

CS: Yes.

UU: *Are the people within these government installations who are working with these entities experiencing such traumas, or are they left alone?*

CS: I don't think that they are experiencing trauma because they need those people as part of the grand deception. Keep in mind, while they're dealing with them on the physical plane they're also actually dealing with an interdimensional phenomenon.

UU: *Like an astral phenomenon?*

CS: Yes...

UU: *...Do you think that the government is dealing with two types of aliens?*

CS: I definitely think that they are dealing with two types of entities, but you've got to keep in mind one thing - the good guys are not going to give us anything to kill our fellow man.

UU: *If you were to see this in an article, is there something that you would like to say?*

"CS: Definitely. 'Shut me up and shut the other people up that are like me. Go ahead and have an unbiased congressional investigation into the UFO matter. Give across the board immunity to any and all service members and civilian government workers who have any knowledge of crashed retrieval aircraft or underground bases to let them come talk freely to a congressional committee on UFOs so that they might talk and clear the air. Get it out that UFOs are a reality. They are here now, they have underground bases. If they go ahead and grant that immunity you'll have people come forth and talk. But they will not talk unless that immunity is granted. Now if I'm wrong - go ahead and offer it, set up a committee, a congressional committee to hear all the evidence, weigh all the facts - then it's a put up or shut up proposition.'

UU: *Why haven't the aliens just simply infiltrated in relation to these government deals.*

"CS: The U.S. government may believe that there's no defense and that they are highly evolved and technologically superior to us. There are those of us, however, that firmly believe - or should I say know - that there are defenses against these folks. In unity there is strength. That strength is derived from knowledge. The knowledge that must be had is the knowledge of the truth. With the truth we can go ahead and combat these entities..."

EXPOSED: THE ULTIMATE DECEPTION
Commander X

At this very moment high level sources in the government are attempting at all costs to keep under careful wraps the biggest military cover-up in United States history. It is a conspiracy that involves a project so hush-hush that only the President and a handful of his most trusted advisors—members of the Defense Department, the CIA and the National Security Council—are even aware of the very existence of this classified above Top Secret matter that could well alter the course of our very lives.

Those in the military, because of their dutiful assignments, who have found about or been confronted with this "secret," often find themselves undergoing intense security clearance checks and personal persecution that extends for years after they have retired, or have been drummed out of the service, because they literally know too much about what is happening.

This secret—which can best be labeled THE ULTIMATE DECEPTION—involves the fact that visitors from outer space have not only set foot on this planet and exchanged scientific data with us, but have been maintaining bases here for many years. Several groups of aliens have actually established ongoing relationships with our leaders. And we have even sent representatives to other worlds, and welcomed with open arms their representatives, who continue to live here under our very noses, under tight security.

It all began in 1947 when a space ship crashed near Roswell, New Mexico and several members of the alien crew were killed in an unfortunate mishap. There is reason, however, to believe that the first pieces of an extraterrestrial craft actually fell into Hitler's hands when he captured a flying disc shortly before the beginning of World War Two.

Flying ace John Lear, son of the founder of the Lear Aircraft Company, who has personally won every FAA flying award ever granted, is among the very few who have managed to break through this stony wall of silence. Due to his "back door" connections with the CIA and other military branches (for whom he has flown various missions) he has met key individuals who realize the full scope of what is going on.

Lear has said—and this confirms information given to me personally by yet other sources—that there are actually several groups of interplanetary visitors coming to Earth. His traveler's guide to the cosmos reads as follows:

Here is a list of some of the probable visitors to earth from outer space. The only known home of these visitors is that of the EBE's and which is Zeta Reticuli 1 and 2, a binary star system visible from the southern hemisphere approximately 38 light years away, with a spectral class of G2, identical to our sun.

Three types of EBE's (Grays): Gray-1: 3-1/2 feet tall. Large head. Large slanted eyes. Worship technology. Don't give a damn about mankind.

Gray-2:Same type, different finger arrangement, slightly different face. More sophisticated than Gray-1 use common sense, passive. May not need secretions.

Gray's: Same basic type. Lips thinner. More subservient to other two grays.

Blondes, Swedes, Nordics:

Known by any of these monikers. Similar to humans. Blond hair, blue eyes. Will not break universal law of "non-interference" to help us. They could only intervene if any Gray activity would have adverse effect in another part of universe.

Inter-dimensional:

Entity that can assume various shapes. Peaceful nature.

Hairy Dwarfs:

four feet tall, 35 lbs. Extremely strong. Hairy. Neutral. Don't try to hurt intelligent life.

The Tall Race:

Look like humans but seven or eight feet tall. United with Blondes.

Humans appearing similar to Blondes seen with grays:

Drones created by Grays. Child-like mentality.

MIB's:

Men in black. Wear all black. Sunglasses. Very pale skin. Do not conform to normally accepted patterns. Extremely sensitive to light. May be holographic image.

When this all started-up until the mid and late 1950s-the government was under the mistaken impression that all the visitors arriving on our celestial shores were friendly toward our still developing civilization. This benevolent "Space Brothers" image is best exemplified in the majority of the contact accounts of this period, such as the stories told by George Adamski and George Van Tassel, in which ordinary citizens were going for rides into space and having telepathic conversations with human-looking space entities.

In fact, even members of the military were apparently enjoying tete-a-tetes with our newly found extraterrestrial friends.

Take this case that is still at least practically locked away somewhere in a hidden file drawer in the basement war room of the Pentagon. Inside this file is perhaps one of the most impressive UFO contact cases of all time—and the incident in question actually involves an Air Force official, the Office of Naval Intelligence, and the CIA.

Until just recently, the entire contents of this manila folder was closely guarded, stamped "TOP SECRET." It's contents were finally leaked to an enterprising scriptwriter, Robert Emenegger, on assignment from Sandier Institutional Films, producers of syndicated news programs. The source of this "leak" was, surprisingly enough, Lt. Col. Robert Friend, USAF, former head of Project Blue Book and a UFO debunker for the government.

Retired now, Robert Friend has done at least a partial "about-face" on UFOs. Not only does he allow for their existence, but he seems to seriously consider even the more bizarre contact stories.

A most revealing interview with Friend—done under cordial circumstances—appears in the book, UFOs, Past, Present and Future. The volume is adapted from the television special of the same name. In this interview, the former Blue Book spokesman describes a case which shows for a fact that the government knows all about the alien's arrival on Earth.

While head of the Air Force's UFO project, Friend says he was informed as a "matter of security" that a well-respected Rear Admiral in the Navy was especially interested in a woman, living in Maine, who claimed to be receiving highly advanced technologically correct information from extraterrestrial beings. These entities were said to contact her while she sat in a trance-like state. The Admiral, with the approval of the Air Force, sent two of his most responsible men to investigate.

Relaxing in a chair before them, the woman expressed her willingness to answer any questions they might pose. At this point, she no longer remained in control of her physical self. Her body was ostensibly "taken over" by members of an intergalactic organization referred to as the "Universal Association of Planets."

A few minutes into the off-beat "conversation," one of the officers present, a Navy commander, was told that further answers would be directed through him. The officer was instructed to hold in his hand a pen lying on a nearby table. The spacemen then took control of his fingers and proceeded to respond to questions through a process known in parapsychological quarters as "automatic writing. "

Lt. Col. Friend notes that news of this highly provocative experiment traveled as fast as a rocket back to Washington. Top brass at the Central Intelligence

Agency got wind of the episode. They demanded to know more. It was Friend's duty to find out what he could.

"It was in 1959," he told researcher Emenegger, "when I was invited to attend a meeting in the security portion of a Washington government building. I was briefed on an experiment that had been conducted with this same Naval commander before a group of CIA members and military personnel. It was described how, after going into a trance, the commander contacted a supposed extraterrestrial being. Several questions were put to him, and answers came back such as: 'Do you favor any government group or race?' Both were "NO." Can we see a spaceship? The commander, still in a trance, told the group to go to the window and they'd have proof. The group went to the window, where they supposedly observed a UFO. I was told that a call was made for a radar confirmation. The reply was that that particular quadrant of the sky was blanked out on radar at that time."

Continuing for the printed pages of UFOs—Past, Present and Future, Friend says that, after being briefed on all the details, he asked the naval officer if the officer could attempt a contact for him personally. While he watched, the commander went into a deep trance. During this period, his Adam's apple is said to have moved up and down more rapidly than is normal.

"Questions were put to him, and he printed the answers in rather large letters, using rapid but jerky motions. It wasn't like a sample of his natural hand. During the course of questioning, we were told the name of some of the so-called extraterrestrials. One was TRILL,' another 'AL-OMAR,' and another 'AFFA,' purportedly from the planet Uranus."

The Blue Book head admits that he was puzzled. "All those involved were found to be highly credible and responsible professional government men." After turning to his report, Friend was told by a superior to forget the entire affair. He was informed that the CIA was making their own study, and therefore the Air Force had been instructed to "lay off."

What was his reaction to this command? As might be expected, it was a military one. "Well, when a general tells a colonel to forget it—I forget it!" The Lt. Col, later discovered that every last witness present in that government building on the day the Naval officer went into trance was relocated or transferred to other duty. "To this day," concludes the ex-Air Force official, "it's an unresolved incident to me. I just don't know what to make of it...."

CRILL, it should be noted, has communicated with others in privileged positions in the government and military, as have other beings with similar sounding names.

Primarily, what the government doesn't want the people to know is that an actual agreement was drawn up between the military and the group which John

AMERICA'S TOP SECRET TREATY WITH ALIEN LIFE FORMS

Lear and others have identified as the EBEs (short for Extraterrestrial Biological Entities). As previously stated, initially the key figures taking part in this scenario had no reason to suspect anything but the best from those they had taken into their confidence. The EBEs said they wanted to take a few humans for examination, that they had actually seeded the planet at the time of creation, eons ago, and simply wanted to keep track of their scientific experiment. For being allowed the privilege of abducting members of the human race on a limited basis, they were seemingly willing to give us scientific data which would greatly enhance our technology. What the government didn't realize is that they planned to abduct tens of thousands of individuals, plant monitoring devices in their brains, and program them with specific series of responses to direct commands.

The EBEs—also behind our backs—began to mutilate cows and other animals because they wished to use their tissues to create a genetically advanced race of flesh and blood robots. When the government realized what the EBEs had in mind, and wanted to back out on their agreement, the aliens took over several of the bases where they had already installed underground laboratories.

Because they are not willing to admit to their mistakes, and due to the fact that they went behind the public's backs in order to conceal this agreement, various members of the military have gone out of their way to keep this matter a closely guarded secret at all costs.

As someone with close military ties, I am in a privileged position to know what state these affairs are currently undergoing. I believe it is my patriotic duty to reveal all that I know regardless of the possible consequences. We live in a great country, a nation that believes in free speech, and I see absolutely no reason why this information shouldn't be divulged, especially before it is too late and while we are still able to stamp out the menace among us.

This conspiracy has gone on far too long, and it surely would continue were it not for a few brave souls who have literally risked their very lives to leak the story of the century to a public who has been left in "blissful ignorance." I can testify to the fact that this conspiracy leads right to the front gate of the White House and behind the walls of the Kremlin; for it is a secret that all the major world powers share, but continue to keep to themselves for fear of what the repercussions of their actions and eventual outcome of the situation may be.

This book is only the first of what I hope will be several volumes devoted to networking the truth about this ongoing situation before it becomes too late. Though this is a legitimate horror story, there is a positive side to it. For yes, indeed, in addition to the EBEs who wish to gain total domination over our planet, there are also benevolent forces arriving from space, who are much more advanced than we are, and who wish to see us develop beyond our current primitive state of being.

This, then, is the story that must be told at ALL COST. In the pages that follow, I wish to share information that has been given to me from "inside sources," which should more-or-less provide a chronicle of the events as they have been taking place for the past several decades, leading right up to the present moment.

Official CIA documents based upon UFO propulsion research being conducted at "secret institutions," provides illustration of how mysterious alien discs fly. Several such discs have been seen airborne near highly classified Groom Lake, Nevada test site.

CRASHED SAUCERS, ALIENS IN CAPTIVITY, AND A COSMIC EXCHANGE PROGRAM

On a nationally broadcast television program that went into an estimated 30 million homes, a government agent—his face cloaked in shadows and his voice altered electronically—boldly declared that on several occasions, UFO pilots have remained behind, while a group of Earthborn have traveled off to the far side of the galaxy in a sort of "cosmic exchange program" that remains classified. This statement was made in total candor. Apparently, one such "swap" took place when a craft made a prearranged landing at an Air Force base in the Southwest. Motion picture footage of this historic event was even taken and the film was due to be released to the world, only to eventually be yanked out of the hands of the producer who had been placed in charge of the production.

In the incidents where UFOs have crashed and the bodies removed from the wreck, most often reliable reports indicate that the pieces of the craft and the corpses themselves have been flown to Wright-Patterson Air Force Base in Dayton, Ohio, where they have been placed into closely guarded quarters. Supposedly, the infamous "Hangar 18" has been the destination over and over again for these alien life forms, and even the likes of Senator Barry Goldwater (who has a higher security clearance than I do), has been refused admission to Hangar 18 after being told that its contents go way beyond a mere Top Secret classification.

Air Force veteran George Ray recently dared anyone on the UFO Echo Computer Bulletin Board to see if they could "get inside of the large black hangar at the back of the base, and after you've seen the inside of it, then come tell me the Air Force doesn't believe in UFOs,"

Ray continued by stating that for the entire time he was in the Air Force (for over 12 years) he only knew of one person who had actually been inside Hangar 18.

"That was because he worked there. It seems that the government did not like the job that the Security Police (AF COPS) were doing so the control of this hangar and surrounding buildings was placed into the hands of the N.S.A. and the Federal Police Agency (supposedly a branch of the U.S. Marshall's Office, under the Dept. of Justice). Anyway, prior to the security exchange this person had to do an inventory. He said that the items that were in those buildings could not be believed. He told me some of what he had seen, but at the time I just blew it off."

Furthermore, Ray says that, "while stationed at an Alert Site in Alaska, we scrambled more than once on objects that were not aircraft. The pilots would not tell us what they saw, yet after every time this happened all aircrews involved were immediately rotated back to the home station. Even when they would wind up back out there with us they would not tell us what they had seen. I know that this happened four times while I was stationed there and I could not tell you how many times total that it has happened. I just have to accept that they saw something that was not of standard aircraft design and until they are allowed to come forward with eyewitness reports, it will continue to be a rumor generating mill."

Of all those in possession of at least some of the facts, one individual stands out as being a "great UFOlogist" working in this field. Robert Barry has for many years been carrying on a crusade to get this important information to the ears and eyes of the public, organizing lectures and seminars from Philadelphia to Cape Canaveral. For the most part, he has been ignored by the UFOlogical community due to his religious and political affiliations and views. An attempt has been made to discredit him, but his important work goes on despite harsh moments that must have made him think of turning his back several times on his chosen task.

Yet, Barry continues non-stop, seeking out reliable sources in the intelligence community who are willing to leak to him the very information we are seeking.

Researcher Barry has made steady inroads getting his "sources" to talk with the promise of anonymity. Many of the things he has learned may seem shocking to those who are uninformed, but they tie in easily with the amazing facts I have managed to secure from other informants.

For instance, Barry confirms that UFO crashes have occurred not only in various parts of the United States, but in other countries, adding fuel to the suspicion that this is an international conspiracy of a gigantic magnitude.

Barry's summary of UFO landings and crashes on U.S. soil are fairly complete, though there have no doubt been others. He has tracked down in many cases the actual witnesses who were there, and gotten them to speak openly about their experiences.

Besides the wreckage found at Roswell (which is probably the site of the best known of all crashes in North America), Barry maintains that the first actual "soft landing" of a space craft probably transpired some 80 miles northeast of Los Angeles at Edwards Air Force Base. This landing took place in full view of President Eisenhower and has been confirmed by others.

Noteworthy is the important military history of the base. Barry states that, "Pilots at Edwards have long tested aircraft and related equipment there. These include supersonic aircraft and the X-15 rocket vehicle. The Experimental Flight Test Center trains pilots and astronauts for our space program there.

"This base was established in 1933 as Muroc Dry Lake and was later renamed for Captain Glen W. Edwards, a test pilot who lost his life in an aircraft crash there in 1948.

"This base, both under the name of Muroc and Edwards, has been the subject of many reports relating to UFOs.

"It was during 1952 that one of Muroc's pilots witnessed something in one of the hangars that completely stunned him. He stood before a strange craft; it was circular, the very kind that had been seen over American cities in earlier months.

"The following morning, this pilot was dispatched on what was to be a routine mission. After the warm-up period was finished, he taxied his plane to the runway for takeoff.

"That was the last anyone ever saw of that pilot and his plane. He vanished along with his aircraft and nothing was ever found to indicate a crash. He simply went, but where, perhaps we will never know!"

One of the first stories to break about a landed UFO and an American President has come from a variety of sources. Allegedly Eisenhower was flown to Muroc Dry Lake Test Facility from Palm Springs, following his being elected in 1952.

"Accordingly, President Eisenhower, after viewing the craft, decided the American public was not yet ready for a disclosure such as this and the discovery remained a top secret.

"Some years ago, I read a report whereby an official notice was circulated throughout Muroc, that nobody on the base would be permitted to leave and those outside the base at the time were not permitted to return until further notice.

"This order remained in effect for a period of three days. The year was around 1954 if my memory serves me correctly. This would have been the general time period of the reported crashed space craft at Muroc." Other countries have not been immune to UFO crashes. They have happened elsewhere from China to Peru.

For example, notes Barry, "Madagascar, an island off the southeastern coast of Africa, was the scene of one such incident, when a UFO exploded and crashed in the marketplace of Fort Dauphin. This crash was confirmed by the Madagascar Interior Ministry and was reported on the government owned Radio Madagascar.

"The craft was cigar-shaped and prior to crashing, it exploded and lit up the entire area. After impact, firemen were dispatched to the scene, and the flames were extinguished. Fortunately, there were no injuries.

"No follow-up reports were released as to what happened to the UFO debris. Radio Madagascar was silent on the subject thereafter. Some of the news of this case leaked off the island and was reported in a New Zealand newspaper on July 22, 1978. Nothing has ever been reported by the U.S. news media regarding this crash."

Likewise, NASA experts probed a reputed fallen object in Bolivia.

"On May 6th, 1978,"states Barry, "a UFO crashed into a hill-side near the Bolivian/Argentine border in desolate country. Upon impact, there was a tremendous explosion that destroyed a portion of the hill. It created an earth tremor causing panic among the Indians inhabiting this area.

"This object was witnessed by many, prior to impact, and the Bolivian government declared the area 'off-limits. NASA experts arrived at the site on May 15th. This crash occurred during the rainy season and caused a delay in reaching the scene of the crash any earlier," notes Barry, who had the opportunity to speak with one of those dispatched to this locale. "This NASA affiliate, a personal friend of mine, told me the U. S. Air Force sent a cargo plane and aboard was a team of experts, including my friend.

"The remains of the object were finally removed and placed aboard the cargo plane and returned to the United States. I was not told where it had been taken, but I was informed that the object was neither an American nor Russian satellite. Since the subject is still classified, I was unable to learn anything more about this incident."

Several other crashes have occurred in China.

"During 1973, a downed space craft impacted on Chinese soil and the following year, one reportedly crashed in a lake. No beings were found at the time of retrieval by the Chinese government, though I was told that there must have been occupants at the time, since there were indications the craft had been manned. What happened to them? No one knows.

"I have been further informed that since 1974, China has done a lot of research work based on the knowledge learned from the crashed saucers, and have managed to duplicate one and fly it!"

As to why the American news media has not reported on these foreign UFO crash cases, one of which involved NASA, Barry maintains that his informant told him, "the United States cannot control the reporting of such cases in foreign countries, but our government can control the influx of foreign reports into our own country by using reasons of national security to keep them out of the press."

As for U.S. reports, Barry claims he knows for a fact that UFOs have crashed in Arizona, California, Kansas, Ohio, and Pennsylvania. "I have spoken with one government UFO investigator on a one-to-one basis, who personally has traveled to the scene of such accidents. We can pretty well be sure that there is, in 'deep freeze,' somewhere between 30 and 34 space alien cadavers being held at a number of our major military bases."

Barry goes so far as to say some aliens survived their crashes. "It is my contention that since we have, on a worldwide basis, so many crashed saucer cases and reported body retrievals, surely in all of this time, not all the aliens died. Surely some did survive!

"New information is beginning to create a crack in the 'national security' wall and a few isolated cases of survival have surfaced. One of these involved a spectacular incident during 1962 when a spacecraft crashed in New Mexico.

"When the UFO was first picked up on military radar crossing the southern United States, indications were that the craft was enduring flight difficulty. This particular section of the United States is a magnetic fault line zone and in turn may give us a clue as to their mode of travel.

"Air Force interceptors were ordered into the air and proceeded to follow the UFO across two states before it came down in New Mexico. No attempt was made to shoot the craft out of the sky.

"As it reached New Mexico air space, it began to lose altitude and coming in low over desert sands, crashed some 80 miles south of Holloman Air Force Base at an estimated speed of 90 miles per hour."

Barry's informant revealed much to him: "He told me the craft was 56 feet in diameter and nearly 15 feet in height. It was the typical Saturn-type, like two plates inverted with a rim and portholes. The underside of the craft was slightly damaged upon impact.

"The landing unit of the craft was not down a the time of the crash, giving an indication its occupants were either dead or not capable of controlling the vehicle.

"New Mexico State Police were dispatched to the isolated crash site and roped the area off. Within the hour, military/government personnel arrived. My informant was on the scene the following morning. Two occupants manned the craft. One was dead; the other was alive but from all indications had been seriously injured in the crash.

"An attempt was made to communicate with the human-like alien. Entry into the ship was gained through a hatch opening located on the lower section near the rim area. A portable tape recorder was used in the attempted communication.

"The alien, described as 42 inches in height, attempted to speak with one of the individuals assigned to the task. The recorder got it all on tape. The alien tried to communicate in a language unknown on this world. The tape was eventually taken to language experts within the highest levels of the government in order to break down the communications barrier.

"A short time later, the little fellow died. Both of the bodies were eventually sent to a university medical hospital located in the mid-Atlantic states"

According to Robert Barry, Hawaii has been the locale for several crashes and survival reports.

"One such incident occurred during the year of 1944, prior to the end of the war. I missed this one by nearly a year since I came through Hawaii by military flight en route home. We landed there and spent 24 hours before continuing on to California.

"This incident involved a space craft that was likewise out of control and crashed in Hawaii. Again, it's the same old story: the military to the rescue. In this particular case, the NAVY CB unit was involved in the retrieval of the craft and its surviving aliens.

"Several of the aliens were reported still alive at the crash site and one military man at the scene personally witnessed the removal of one live alien from the crashed craft.

"What happened to them from this point is not known, but without doubt, they were taken to a Naval Hospital where attempts at saving their lives undoubtedly occurred and if successful,the next move would have been attempted communication."

A UFO crashed in Louisiana and a memo in the handwriting of FBI Director J, Edgar Hoover shows that his agents knew all about it, but were kept from the scene by the Army, who had gotten there first. In 1953 the military was on scheduled maneuvers when Barry says the unexpected took place.

"Without warning, a space vehicle plunged to earth from the heavens, startling the soldiers who were a short distance away.

'The command was given to encircle the craft and block the area off to anyone except those directly involved in the maneuver. Military ambulances were dispatched to the crash site. Upon arrival, medics went to work removing one of the alien bodies. It was placed on a stretcher and removed to the ambulance. This being was presumed dead.

"A short distance away, another ambulance crew converged on three surviving aliens and escorted them to the waiting ambulance at which time they were immediately whisked away to an unknown destination.

"We are assuming that the first alien died at the crash site, but there is the possibility it was simply unconscious, and regained consciousness later.

"But the main point to be made here, is that there were THREE KNOWN alien survivors who were injured to the point that they needed only to be helped to the waiting ambulance, at which time they were immediately removed from the scene.

"What happened to them? Where were they taken? Did all three later die? Is it possible that two of them or perhaps even one, survived and remains alive today? If so, what have authorities learned about the creature?"

Up until recently, news from Poland was censored, yet probably one of the most detailed descriptions of a crashed UFO transpired on February 21, 1959, when dock workers in the Polish port of Gdynia witnessed a brilliant UFO plunge into the harbor basin.

"Port authorities dispatched three skin divers to the scene. The divers descended into the icy water and were hindered by a thick layer of mud. Despite this factor, one of them retrieved a piece of metal which was later examined by the Polish Navy as well as the Gdynia Polytechnic University. No information was released as to the findings made by either group," Barry continues.

"Several days after the crash, harbor men guarding the beaches, sighted a strange being, a man dragging himself, appearing to be totally exhausted. As the guards approached the creature, they discovered that part of its face and hair appeared to be burned. The alien spoke no known language during an attempted communication between it and the guards. The being was then removed to the university hospital where it was isolated and examined.

"A problem arose when examining physicians realized there was no opening... no buttons. .. no zipper..,on its uniform. The uniform was not of ordinary material such as wool, but of some type of metallic-like substance which had to be cut open by means of special instruments and with a great deal of effort!

"The doctors were shocked. They discovered the alien's organs were MUCH different from ours; the blood system was totally new and unknown to them, and the number of fingers differed from people born on this world.

"The humanoid remained alive until a kind of arm band was removed. When this was done, the creature died. His body was sent to the Soviet Union for further examination."

From other sources we have been told about aliens who are freely living among us, who are communicating with our officials on a daily basis.

In June of 1978, Bob Barry was talking on the telephone with a good friend who has been with the government since the 1950s and deeply involved in UFO investigations all that time.

"We were discussing cybernetics, a science dealing with the comparative study of the operations of complex electronic computers and the human nervous system. Part of our conversation involved human-like beings with cybernetic equipment.

"My source momentarily strayed from this subject and told me about his involvement in a case where an attempt was made to communicate with a humanoid.

"This attempted communication with a live space alien took place during 1965. The alien could read my friend's mind and know everything he was thinking. He attempted to pick up the thoughts of the alien, but failed.

"Realizing what I was being told, I immediately asked him if the alien was from a crashed spacecraft or if not, what was behind it all. My friend then realized, too late, what he had said, admitted it was strictly an accident, a slip due to the topic we had just been discussing."

In yet another case that took place in the western Sierra Madre mountains of Mexico, Barry says his sources reveal that several small alien-type, humanoid beings dressed in luminous uniforms, emerged from the crash site.

"Nearly 200 soldiers from the Mexican Army searched for what was described as 'several of the crew' that survived the impact. Two of the aliens reportedly died later. This report was carried by the foreign press in South America, but the U.S. news media was again silent."

C.M. Tenney had just turned 80 in 1981 when Barry spoke to the retired businessman who resided in Delta, Colorado.

"It was during 1953, and Mr. Tenney was operating a flower shop in Conrad, Montana, about 40 miles northwest of Great Falls. Part of his weekly routine was that of making frequent trips to Great Falls to secure flowers for his business,

"One morning, while en route to Great Falls on one of these trips, Tenney saw what appeared to be smoke emanating from the vicinity of a nearby mountain. Since forest fires are common there, he passed it off and gave it no further thought.

"The following day, however, something unusual happened that caused him to have second thoughts about this incident. He was returning to his flower shop from Great Falls and was driving along the highway between Dutton and Brady (Montana), when he sighted a cigar-shaped object that appeared to be pulsating.

"The object was off to the left and appeared to be some 200 feet above the ground level. Without warning, the UFO began discharging what he described as fireballs that landed on both sides as well as directly in the middle of the highway.

"The fireballs quickly extinguished themselves, at which time the UFO increased its speed and vanished into the heavens, leaving behind a man as white as a ghost with his hair standing on edge.

"Tenney stopped in Brady to see a friend and related his frightening encounter. This incident was reported to the Montana State Police and by the time he arrived home, he had a telephone call waiting from the Malmstrom Air Force Base near Great Falls.

"They wanted him to drive there immediately. He told them he couldn't make it since he had to prepare flowers for a funeral scheduled for the next day. He was told to be at the base the next morning at ten o'clock or they would send Air Force

Police for him. He was there at ten the next morning!

"He was met by three men, one an Air Force officer who led him to the office of a colonel on the second floor of a building totally isolated from all other buildings at the base. This building contained no windows and was surrounded by a high wire fence.

"He was instructed to keep his eyes straight ahead and not do any looking around en route to the office. Tenney saw officers carrying packages marked TOP SECRET.'

"In the colonel's office, he was grilled extensively about his experience. His interview was typed and he had to sign a copy in the presence of a notary at the base.

"When completed, four officials then led Tenney down the stairs leading to the front door of this 'jail-like building.' As they neared the door, two men 'staggering in with large laundry bags' were showing signs of difficulty in carrying the contents because of their weight.

"One of the Air Force men accidentally dropped the bag he was carrying in front of Tenney. He was shocked. 'I could make out the outline of a body. It appeared to be doubled up,' he said. Tenney saw its head, knees and feet.

"The two men grabbed me and the officer opened the door and they threw me out,' Tenney stated. He added that the officer yelled at him to get out of the building immediately.

"His conclusion regarding this entire affair was that the smoke he had seen in the mountain range was caused by a crashed space-craft, and the UFO he saw the following day was another ship in search of its downed companion. To him, the two laundry bags represented two bodies from the crashed vehicle. From what we learned, he just might be right in his theory."

But the story is not over, as another—a second UFO—was sighted the day following his visit to the Air Force base. "It occurred while he was en route to the greenhouse to get floral supplies. It was a brilliant silver-colored object high in the sky.

"The UFO came in low over the area, moving towards the nearby mountains and eventually disappearing.

'Tenney reached a decision then and there that he was going to remain silent. He wanted no more third degree grilling from anyone, anywhere! Yes, Tenney might have hit the 'nail on the head' with his thinking on the entire series of events!"

Trying to pin down hard evidence of all of this may not be easy to come by, but it does exist if we dare dig deep enough—even photographic evidence!

"I was told that a newsman for a Florida television station reportedly had, or at one time was in possession of, a picture of a downed spacecraft.

"This picture was allegedly taken by one of the guards assigned to guard 'Building 18' (Hangar 18) at Wright-Patterson Air Force Base, during the time a UFO was housed there.

"While I was lecturing on the subject in Florida a few years ago, I attempted to make contact with this man. He was not in at that moment and I left word as to who I was and what I wanted to discuss with him. He never returned the call. Further attempts to reach him have also failed. It is as though he didn't want to discuss the subject with anyone at anytime."

Of course, I don't think I need to confirm that there have been other reported crashes which have been brought to our attention from other sources independent of Mr. Barry's fine research. There may have, for example, been a crash near Lake Panache in northwestern Ontario, Canada, which is just now coming to light due to the concentrated investigative work of Diane Payton, who confirms an account given by Edward T. Thomas, a successful draftsman and UFO researcher who in July of 1961 was on vacation with his wife in the area.

Payton's dramatic report goes as follows;

"Several days after arriving at their rented cabin on the lake the Thomas' met a local couple, Ernie and Geraldine Moven, the owners of a small grocery and dry goods store. When the subject of UFOs was brought into the conversation, Ernie Moven told of a man who had claimed to have seen a 'flying boxcar' crash into the lake about six weeks earlier.

"It seemed this man, a then recently arrived transient known only as Charlie, had told his story to a group of men at the local tavern, and had tried, unsuccessfully, to trade pieces of metal he said were from the object for drinks. Everyone had had a good laugh, and Charlie was eventually pitched out of the establishment on his ear.

"Mr. Thomas had some difficulty tracing Charlie to a small lodge a short distance around the lake. He was doing clean up and other odd jobs around the cabins and grounds, and was sleeping in a converted store room next to the kitchen.

"Mr. Thomas described Charlie as a thoroughly disreputable appearing man in his middle fifties, illiterate and alcoholic. It was not a simple matter to persuade him to talk about the 'flying box-car.' However, he agreed to tell his story in exchange for a bottle of bourbon the Thomas' had in their cabin.

"Charlie claimed he had been sleeping on a porch of one of a group of unoccupied cabins at the northern end of the lake when, at dawn, he was awakened by a terrific roaring noise. An object like a 'big gray boxcar' came angling down from the sky with fire streaming from the rear and 'licks of flame on the top.' It appeared to be moving in jerks, and the front end was bobbing up and down. Before crashing into the lake with a great splash and clouds of steam, it sent out a spray of glowing sparks from the underside near the tail.

"Some of the 'sparks' landed on rocks at the water's edge; the rest fell into the lake. To Charlie, some distance away, the rocks looked as though they had been splashed with 'spots of bright gold.' Apparently he had the notion that what looked like gold (hot and glowing), actually was gold. For when the normal stillness and silence had returned to the lake, he claimed he wasted no time hurrying down to 'gather some up.' There was no further sign of the UFO.

"There is no description of the amount of metal on the rocks, other than 'some.' Although it turned out to be silver in color rather than gold as Charlie had expected, he thought it might still have some value, so he proceeded to collect pieces of it. The larger ones went into his pockets, the smaller into a rusty two-pound coffee can which had been in a pile of trash nearby. Most of the metal was adhering to the rocks in thin patches. When battered with a stone it broke into small irregular fragments.

"Charlie could not recall what happened to the larger chunks of the metal, but he had hidden the coffee can under his bed. This he offered to Mr. Thomas at a price. Mr. Thomas was understandably reluctant to accept the story, but he decided to do so, and purchased the can of metal after examining it, and after securing a promise from Charlie that he would take him to the exact place where the incident supposedly occurred, Charlie was to be paid for guiding Mr. Thomas to the spot!! Arrangements were made to rent a boat for the trip the following morning.

"When Mr. Thomas went to the lodge where Charlie had been staying, he found the man had moved out, apparently during the night. No one knew exactly when he had left, or that he had left at all. Mr. Thomas was unable to trace him. No one else in the area knew anything about the alleged UFO crash. No one had seen or heard anything out of the ordinary. Mr. Thomas hired a guide and spent the remainder of his vacation, four days, searching the northern coastline of the lake. There were several groups of cabins which had been unoccupied at the time of Charlie's alleged sighting. But, no evidence of any kind was found to support the story. No further investigation was made at that time.

"Mr. Thomas believed he must have been the victim of a hoax, The NICAP group concurred when they were told of the incident two years later, though two serious members made a special trip to visit the area in the summer of 1964. At that date no one remembered either Mr. Thomas, or Charlie, and nothing could be learned. Ernie Moven recalled 'something about someone who was searching for something in the lake,' but that was all.

"In 1968 Edward Thomas, then 74, died of a heart attack. His wife had no interest in UFOs, and gave her husband's collection of material to the NICAP group. Included were the metal fragments, still in the original coffee can. About two dozen of the best specimens were sorted out to be retained in the group's permanent file. The rest were divided among any of the members who wanted them.

"The arguments against the 'validity' of the incident are obvious. However, there are two main points in favor of it. The first is this: Consider Charlie. Could an individual of this type make up such a story?

"And the second: More tangible? The metal. It was analyzed, and was found to be a rather unusual alloy. Not the kind of thing which could be picked up in the Canadian woods. No one knew where Charlie came from before he appeared at lake Panache. But it would be extremely unlikely (though not impossible, of course) for him to have had access to the type of area where such metal could be found. That is some sort of specialized manufacturing or metallurgical research facility working with the light metals associated with experimental aircraft, certain scientific apparatus, and pure research."

The most recent UFO crash and retrieval known to this author took place in South Africa in May, 1989. According to investigator Bill Knell of Island Skywatch, who is in charge of releasing information in the U.S., his organization was originally contacted regarding this matter by representatives of Quest International, a British-based UFO organization. "The fact that Quest is primarily made up of retired military and police officials of good standing weighed heavily in our decision to become the ONLY American group authorized to print or distribute these materials."

Supposedly the UFO was coming in over the Kalahari Desert when it was shot down by a specially equipped Mirage S.A. Air Force jet. Through special arrangements the crashed object, its occupants, and all materials related to the crash were brought to the U.S.

A "CLASSIFIED TOP SECRET-DO NOT DIVULGE" FILE FROM THE SOUTH AFRICAN AIR FORCE READS THUSLY.

Case History

At 13:45 GMT on 7 May 1989 the naval frigate radioed Cape Town naval headquarters to report an unidentified flying object that appeared on radar scopes, heading towards the African continent in a northwesterly direction at a calculated speed of 5,745 nautical miles per hour. Naval headquarters acknowledged and confirmed that object was also tracked by airborne radar, military ground radar installations and D. F. Malan International Airport at Cape Town. The object entered South African air space at 13:52 GMT. Radio contact was attempted with object, but all communications to the object proved futile. Valhalla Air Force Base was notified and two armed Mirage fighters were scrambled. The object suddenly changed course at great speed, which would be impossible for military aircraft to duplicate. At 13:59 GMT squadron leader reported that they had radar and visual confirmation of the object. The order was given to arm and fire the experimental aircraft mounted Thor 2 laser cannon at object. This was done. Squadron leader reported that several blinding flashes emanated from the object. The object started wavering whilst still heading in a northerly direction. At 14:02 it was reported that the object was decreasing altitude at a rate of 3,000 feet per minute. Then at great speed it dived at an angle of 25 degrees and impacted in desert terrain 80 km north of South African border with Botswana, identified as the Central Kalahari Desert. Squadron leader was instructed to circle the area until a retrieval of the object was complete. A team of Air Force intelligence officers, together with medical and technical staff, were promptly taken to area of impact for investigation and retrieval. The findings were as follows: 1)A crater of 150 metres in diameter and 12 metres in depth.

1) A silver coloured disc-shaped object 45 degrees embedded in side of crater.

2) 3) Around object sand and rocks were fused together by the intense heat.

4) An intense magnetic and radioactive environment around object resulted in electronic failure in Air Force equipment.

5) It was suggested by team leader that object be moved to a classified Air Force base for further investigation and this was done. The terrain of impact was filled with sand and rubble to disguise all evidence of this event having ever taken place.

Despite the force of its impact upon the Earth, as amazing as it may be, at least one alien was found alive onboard the crippled UFO. The South Africans—as part of a little known treaty agreement made between the two countries—turned over the wounded survivor to the American military. Though it may be hard to swallow, the alien ended up—of all places–as a "guest" at Wright-Patterson Air Force Base in Dayton, Ohio (home of the infamous Hangar 18).

When the base commander (who was said to be in charge of this "special guest") came to the phone, the high-ranking military man seemed truly shocked that anyone should know about the incident, much less the fact that one of the EBEs had gotten out of the wreckage alive. Hesitating for a moment before avoiding the questions put to him, the top brass refused to make any sort of statement, outside of saying that he had "No comment!" to make. Then he hung up!

The case is still under investigation, and hopefully I will be able to check on it a bit more through my own "contacts." Perhaps I will have a more complete report at some future date.

If the past repeats itself—as if often does–other crashes will come to light and some of the doomed objects may contain surviving aliens.

BEHIND THE MASK OF JOHN LEAR

One can't help but be impressed with the name John Lear. After all, his father, William was the famous aviation pioneer who built the Lear Aircraft Company, which today holds down many defense contacts and employs thousands.

Lear—the son—is also highly regarded in aviation circles, having flown a variety of over 150 test aircraft, and having won every award granted by the Federal Aviation Administration.

Until two or three years ago, John Lear had little or no interest in UFOs-he hadn't thought terribly much about the subject, which seemed "way out" to him. Then he chanced to talk to a friend who had been stationed in England when a UFO touched down at a military complex there, and was seen by U.S. servicemen on duty—small creatures and all. Intrigued, Lear began asking around and found some of his former associates in the CIA–for whom he had flown any number of missions–willing to confirm that government leaders knew a great deal more about UFOs, and space aliens than the public was being let on.

Lear discovered to his utter amazement that the U.S. military actually possessed craft from outer space, some of the vehicles were even in partial working order. Apparently, the Americans had initially gotten their hands on these extraterrestrial disc-shaped devices as far back as the late 1940s, upon recovery of the wreckage of a downed saucer that the Nazi's had somehow captured during World War II. Apparently, some of the lethal "death weapons" we subsequently developed were based on facets of this interplanetary technology.

Furthermore, Lear believes any number of flying discs "fell" into our hands when they crashed in the southwest in the late 1940s and early 50s. Scattered around the various crash sites were the bodies of small humanoid beings, the EBEs. At least one alien was found still alive and he, along with his badly burned buddies, were flown to Wright-Patterson Air Force Base in Dayton, Ohio, home of the infamous "Hangar 18"; this final destination the so-called "Blue Room," which the likes of Senator Barry Goldwater has not even been permitted to penetrate.

AMERICA'S TOP SECRET TREATY WITH ALIEN LIFE FORMS

Lear's scenario also includes the suspicion that the government has made secret deals with aliens, actually exchanging humans for advanced technical data. Supposedly, the government was to be provided a list of those being abducted so they could maintain a vigil over them after their experience to make sure that they were not being harmed in any way. Unfortunately, the aliens took advantage of the situation, taking away tens of thousands for God knows what purpose, and implanting small transmitters inside their brains which can be activated for some sinister "mission" at some prearranged future moment.

As the following "briefing paper" from Lear states, the aliens have seized underground facilities on military bases in Nevada and New Mexico, where they are busily putting together a sort of Frankenstein Army—part alien, part human. The military has tried to fight back, but has been repeatedly overpowered. Some 65 CIA agents were reportedly shot to death when they attempted to "take back" one of these bases. The recent end to the "Cold War" even fits nicely into the Lear scenario, in that the Russian and the U.S. military are secretly on the same side, having "teamed up" to fight the menace from space, putting aside their previous differences. "Star Wars" is even part of this battle for control of Earth, meant not to be used against the USSR, but against the saucers should the EBEs try to take total control of the planet any time soon.

According to friend and foe alike, John Lear wears a variety of masks. Sometimes what he has to say seems to lack credibility, but just when you think you've caught him with his jump suit down, evidence pops up that what he has to say may not be so totally off the wall. For example, others with military connections have recently come forward to verify part of his amazing saga, so perhaps it's best to let Lear give his own account of this very bewildering situation that threatens to pit Earth against alien invaders.

The United States Government has been in business with little gray extra-terrestrials for about 20 years. The first truth stated here got Giordano Bruno burned at the stake in AD 1600 for daring to propose that it was real. The second truth has gotten far more people killed trying to state it publicly than will ever be known. But the truth must be told. The fact that the Earth revolves around the sun was successfully suppressed by the church for over 200 years. It eventually caused a major upheaval in the church, government, thought and a realignment of social and traditional values. That was in the 1800's. Now, about 400 years after the first truth was pronounced we must again face the shocking facts. The "horrible truth" the government has been hiding from us over 40 years. Unfortunately, the "horrible truth" is far more horrible than the government ever imagined. In its effort to protect democracy, our government sold us to the aliens. And here is how it happened.

But before I begin, I'd like to offer a word in the defense of those who bargained us away. They had the best of intentions. Germany may have recovered a flying saucer as early as 1939. General James H, Doolittle went to Sweden in 1946 to inspect a flying saucer that had crashed there in Spitzbergen. The horrible truth was known by only a very few persons:

They were indeed ugly little creatures, shaped like praying mantises and who were more advanced than us by perhaps a billion years.

Of the original group that were the first to learn the "horrible truth," several committed suicide, the most prominent of which was General James V. Forrestal who jumped to his death from a 16th story hospital window. General Forrestal's medical records are sealed to this day. President Truman quickly put a lid on the secret and turned the screws so tight that the general public still thinks that flying saucers are a joke. Have I ever got a surprise for them.

In 1947, President Truman established a group of 12 of the top military and scientific personnel of their time. They were known as MJ-12. Although the group exists today, none of the original members are still alive. The last one to die was Gordon Gray, former Secretary of the Army, in 1984. As each member passed away, the group itself appointed a new member to fill the position.

There is some speculation that the group known as MJ-12 expanded to at least several more members. There were several more saucer crashes in the late 1940's, one in Roswell, New Mexico, one in Aztec, New Mexico, and one near Laredo, Texas, about 30 miles inside the Mexican border. Consider, if you will, the position of the United States Government at that time. They proudly thought of themselves as the most powerful nation on Earth, having recently produced the atomic bomb, an achievement so stupendous, it would take Russia 4 years to catch up, and only with the help of traitors to Democracy. They had built a jet aircraft that had exceeded the speed of sound in flight. They had built jet bombers with intercontinental range that could carry weapons of enormous destruction. The post war era, and the future seemed bright.

Now imagine what it was like for those same leaders, all of whom had witnessed the panic of Orson Wells' radio broadcast, The War of the Worlds, in 1938. Thousands of Americans panicked at a realistically presented invasion of Earth by beings from another planet. Imagine their horror as they actually viewed the dead bodies of these frightening looking little creatures with enormous eyes, reptilian skin and claw like fingers. Imagine their shock as they attempted to determine how these strange "saucers" were powered and could discover no part even remotely similar to components they were familiar with: no cylinders or pistons, no vacuum tubes or turbines or hydraulic actuators.

It is only when you fully understand the overwhelming helplessness the government was faced with in the late 40's that you can comprehend their perceived need for a total, thorough, and sweeping cover up, to include the use of "deadly force." The cover-up was so successful that as late as 1985 a senior scientist with the Jet Propulsion Laboratory in Pasadena, California, Dr. Al Hibbs, would look at a video tape of an enormous flying saucer and state for the record, "I'm not going to assign anything to that (UFO) phenomena without a lot more data," Dr. Hibbs was looking at the naked emperor and saying, "He certainly looks naked, but that doesn't prove he's naked."

In July of 1952,a panicked government watched helplessly as a squadron of "flying saucers" flew over Washington, D.C., and buzzed the White House, the Capitol Building, and the Pentagon. It took all the imagination and intimidation the government could muster to force that incident out of the memory of the public.

Thousands of sightings occurred during the Korean war and several more saucers were retrieved by the Air Force. Some were stored at Wright-Patterson Air Force Base, some were stored at Air Force bases near the locations of the crash sites. One saucer was so enormous and the logistic problems in transportation so enormous that it was buried at the crash sight and remains there today.

The stories are legendary on transporting crashed saucers over long distances, moving only at night, purchasing complete farms, slashing through forests, blocking major highways, sometimes driving 2 and 3 lo-boys in tandem with an extraterrestrial load a hundred feet in diameter.

On April 30, 1964, the first communication between these aliens and the U.S. Government took place at Holloman Air Force Base in New Mexico. Three saucers landed at a prearranged area and a meeting was held between the aliens and intelligence officers of the U.S. Government.

During the period of 1969-1971, MJ-12, representing the U.S. Government, made a deal with these creatures, called EBE's (Extraterrestrial Biological Entities, named by Detley Bronk, original MJ-12 member and 6th President of Johns Hopkins University).

The "deal" was that in exchange for "technology" that they would provide to us, we agreed to "ignore" the abductions that were going on and suppress information on the cattle mutilations. The EBE's assured MJ-12 that the abductions (usually lasting about 2 hours) were merely the ongoing monitoring of developing civilizations. In fact, the purposes for the abductions turned out to be:

(1)The insertion of a 3mm spherical device through the nasal cavity of the abductee into the brain. The device is used for the biological monitoring, tracking, and control of the abductee.

(2) Implementation of Posthypnotic Suggestion to carry out a specific activity during a specific time period, the actuation of which will occur within the next two to five years.

(3) Termination of some people so that they could function as living sources

for biological material and substances.

(4) Termination of individuals who represent a threat to the continuation of their activity.

(5) Effect genetic engineering experiments.

(6) Impregnation of human females and early termination of pregnancies to secure the crossbreed infant. The U.S. Government was not initially aware of the far-reaching consequences of their "deal." They were led to believe that the abductions were essentially benign and since they figured the abductions would probably go on anyway whether they agreed or not, they merely insisted that a current list of abductees be submitted, on a periodic basis, to MJ-12 and the National Security Council.

Does this sound incredible? An actual list of abductees sent to the National Security Council? Read on, because I have news for you. The EBE's have a genetic disorder in that their digestive system is atrophied and not functional. Some speculate that they were involved in some type of accident or nuclear war, or possibly on the back side of an evolutionary genetic curve. In order to sustain themselves they use an enzyme or hormonal secretion obtained from the tissue that they extract from humans and animals. (Note: Cows and Humans are genetically similar. In the event of a national disaster, cow's blood can be used by humans.)

The secretions obtained are then mixed with hydrogen peroxide and applied on the skin by spreading or dipping parts of their bodies in the solution. The body absorbs the solution, then excretes the waste back through the skin. The cattle mutilations that were prevalent throughout the period from 1973 to 1983 and publicly noted through newspaper and magazine stories and included a documentary produced by Linda Howe for the Denver CBS affiliate KMGH-TV, were for the collection of these tissues by the aliens. The mutilations included genitals taken, rectums cored out to the colon, eyes, tongue, and throat all surgically removed with extreme precision. In some cases the incisions were made by cutting between the cells, a process we are not yet capable of performing in the field. In many of the mutilations there was no blood found at all in the carcass, yet there was no vascular collapse of the internal organs.

This has been also noted in the human mutilations, one of the first of which was Sgt. Jonathan P. Louette at the White Sands Missile Test Range in 1956, who was found three days after an Air Force Major had witnessed his abduction by a disk shaped object at 0300 while on a search for missile debris downrange. His genitals had been removed, rectum cored out in a surgically precise "plug" up to the colon, eyes removed and all blood removed with, again, no vascular collapse.

From some of the evidence it is apparent that this surgery is accomplished, in most cases, while the victim, animal or human, is still alive. The various parts of the body are taken to various underground laboratories, one of which is known to be near the small New Mexico town of Dulce. This jointly occupied (CIA-Alien) facility has been described as enormous, with huge tiled walls that "go on forever,"

Witnesses have reported huge vats filled with amber liquid with parts of human bodies being stirred inside.

After the initial agreement, Groom Lake, one of this nation's most secret test centers, was closed for a period of about a year, sometime between about 1972 and 1974, and a huge underground facility was constructed for and with the help of the EBE's. The "bargained for" technology was set in place but could only be operated by the EBE's themselves. Needless to say, the advanced technology could not be used against the EBE's themselves, even if needed. During the period between 1979 and 1983 it became increasingly obvious to MJ-12 that things were not going as planned. It became known that many more people (in the thousands) were being abducted than were listed on the official abduction lists. In addition it became obvious that some, not all, but some of the nation's missing children had been used for secretions and other parts required by the aliens.

In 1979 there was an altercation of sorts at the Dulce laboratory. A special armed forces unit was called in to try and free a number of our people trapped in the facility, who had become aware of what was really going on. According to one source, 66 of the soldiers were killed and our people were not freed. By 1984, MJ-12 must have been in stark terror at the mistake they had made in dealing with the EBE's. They had subtly promoted Close Encounters of the Third Kind and E.T. to get the public used to "odd looking" aliens that were compassionate, benevolent and very much our "space brothers." MJ-12 "sold" the EBE's to the public, and were now faced with the fact that quite the opposite was true. In addition, a plan was formulated in 1968 to make the public aware of the existence of aliens on earth over the next 20 years to be culminated with several documentaries to be released during 1985-1987 period of time.

These documentaries would explain the history and intentions of the EBE's. The discovery of the "Grand Deception" put the entire plans, hopes and dreams of MJ-12 into utter confusion and panic. Meeting at the "Country Club," a remote lodge with private golf course, comfortable sleeping and working quarters, and its own private airstrip built by and exclusively for the members of MJ-12, it was a factional fight of what to do now. Part of MJ-12 wanted to confess the whole scheme and shambles it had become to the public, beg their forgiveness and ask for their support. The other part (and majority) of MJ-12 argued that there was no way they could do that, that the situation was untenable and there was no use in exciting the public with the "horrible truth" and that the best plan was to continue the development of a weapon that could be used against the EBE's under the guise of "SDI," the Strategic Defense Initiative, which had nothing whatsoever to do with a defense for inbound Russian nuclear missiles.

As these words are being written, Dr. Edward Teller, "father" of the H-Bomb, is personally in the test tunnels of the Nevada Test Site, driving his workers and associates in the words of one, "like a man possessed." And well he should, for Dr. Teller is a member of MJ-12 along with Dr. Kissinger, Admiral Bobby Inman, and possibly Admiral Poindexter, to name a few of the current members of MJ-12. Before the "Grand Deception" was discovered and accord-ing to a meticulous plan of metered release of information to the public, several documentaries and video tapes were made.

William Moore, a Burbank, California, based UFO researcher who wrote The Roswell Incident, a book published in 1980 that detailed the crash, recovery and subsequent cover-up of a UFO with four alien bodies, has a videotape of two newsmen interviewing a military officer associated with MJ-12. This military officer answers questions relating to the history of MJ-12 and the cover-up, the recovery of a number of flying saucers and the existence of a live alien (one of three living aliens captured and designated, or named, EBE-1, EBE-2, and EBE-3, being held in a facility designated as YY-I1 at Los Alamos, New Mexico. The only other facility of this type, which is electromagnetically secure, is at Edwards Air Force Base in Mojave, California). The officer names those previously mentioned plus a few others: Harold Brown, Richard Helms, Gen. Vernon Walters, JPL's Dr. Lew Allen and Dr. Theodore von Karman, to name a few of the current and past members of MJ-12. The officer also relates the fact that the EBE's claim to have created Christ.

The EBE's have a type of recording device that has recorded all of Earth's history and can display it in the form of a hologram. This hologram can be filmed but because of the way holograms work does not come out very clear on movie film or video tape. The crucifixion of Christ on the Mount of Olives has allegedly been put on film to show the public.

The EBE's claim to have created Christ, which, in view of the "Grand Deception," could be an effort to disrupt traditional values for undetermined reasons. Another video tape allegedly in existence is an interview with an EBE. Since EBE's communicate telepathically, an Air Force Colonel serves as an interpreter.

Just before the recent stock market correction in October of 1987, several newsmen, including Bill Moore, had been invited to Washington, D.C.,to personally film the EBE in a similar type interview, and distribute the film to the public. Apparently, because of the correction in the market, it was felt the timing was not propitious. In any case, it certainly seems like an odd method to inform the public of extraterrestrials, but it would be in keeping with the actions of a panicked organization who at this point in time doesn't know which way to turn.

Moore is also in possession of more Aquarius documents, a few pages of which leaked out several years ago and detailed the supersecret NSA project which had been denied by them until just recently. In a letter to Senator John Glenn, NSA's Director of Policy, Julia B. Wetzel, wrote, "Apparently there is or was an Air Force project with that name (Aquarius)which dealt with UFO's. Coincidentally, there is also an NSA project by that name." NSA's project Aquarius deals specifically with the "communications with the aliens" (the EBE's). Within the Aquarius program was project Snowbird, a project to test fly a recovered alien aircraft at Groom Lake, Nevada. This project continues today at that location.

In the words of an individual who works at Groom Lake, "Our people are much better at taking things apart than they are at putting them back together," Moore, who claims he has a contact with MJ-12, feels that they have been stringing him along, slipping him documents and providing him leads, promising to go public with some of the information on extraterrestrials by the end of 1987. Certain of Moore's statements lead one to believe that Moore himself is a government agent working for MJ-12, not to be strung along, but string along ever hopeful UFOlogists that the truth is just around the corner.

Consider: 1. Moore states emphatically that he is not a government agent, although when Lee Graham (a Southern California based UFOlogist) was investigated by DIS (Defense Investigative Service) for possession of classified documents received from Moore, Moore himself was not. 2. Moore states emphatically that the cattle mutilations of 1973-1983 were a hoax by Linda Howe (producer of A Strange Harvest) to create publicity for herself. He cites the book Mute Evidence as the bottom line of the hoax. Mute Evidence was a government sponsored book to explain the mutilations in conventional terms. 3. Moore states that the U.S.A.F. Academy physics book, Introductory Space Science, vol. I1 chapter 13, entitled "Unidentified Flying Objects," which describes four of the most commonly seen aliens (one of which is the EBE) was written by Lt. Col. Edward R. Theriomas and Major Donald B. Carpenter, Air Force personnel who did not know what they were talking about and were merely siting "crackpot" references. He, Moore, states that the book was withdrawn to excise the chapter.

If the government felt they were being forced to acknowledge the existence of aliens on Earth because of the overwhelming evidence such as the October and November sightings in Wytheville, Va., and recently released books such as Night Siege (Hynek, J. Allen; Imbrogno, Phillip J.; Pratt, Bob: Ballantine Books, Random House, New York),and taking into consideration the "grand deception" and obviously hostile intentions of the EBE's, it might be expedient for MJ-12 to admit the EBE's but conceal the information on the mutilations and abductions. If MJ-12 and Moore were in some kind of agreement then it would be beneficial to Moore to toe the party line. For example, MJ-12 would say..."here are some more genuine documents, but remember, no talking about the mutilations or abductions." This would be beneficial to Moore as it would supply the evidence to support his theory that E.T.'s exist but deny the truths about the E.T.'s. However, if

AMERICA'S TOP SECRET TREATY WITH ALIEN LIFE FORMS

Moore was indeed working for MJ-12, he would follow the party line anyway... admitting the E.T.'s but pooh poohing the mutilations and abductions.

Now you ask, "Why haven't I heard about any of this?"

Who do you think you would hear it from? Dan Rather? Tom Brokaw? Sam Donaldson?

Wrong. These people just read the news, they don't find it. They have ladies who call and interview witnesses and verify statements on stories coming over the wire (either AP or UPI). It's not like Dan Rather would go down to Wytheville, Virginia, and dig into why there were four thousand reported sightings in October and November of 1987. Better that Tom Brokaw or someone else should risk their credibility on this type of story. Tom Brokaw? Tom wants Sam Donaldson to risk his credibility. No one, but no one, is going to risk their neck on such outlandish ideas, regardless of how many people report sightings of 900 foot objects running them off the road,

In the case of the Wytheville sightings, dozens of vans with NASA lettered on the side failed to interest newsmen. And those who asked questions were informed that NASA was doing a weather survey. Well then, you ask, what about our scientists? What about Carl Sagan? Isaac Asimov? Arthur C. Clarke? Wouldn't they have known? If Carl Sagan knows then he is committing a great fraud through the solicitation of memberships in the Planetary Society, "to search for extraterrestrial intelligence. "

Another charade into which the U.S. Government dumps millions of dollars every year is the radio telescope in Arecibo, Puerto Rico, operated by Cornell University with—guess who?—Carl Sagan. Cornell is ostensibly searching for signals from Outer Space, a sign maybe, that somebody is out there. It is hard to believe that relatively intelligent astronomers like Sagan could be so ignorant. What about Isaac Asimov? Surely the most prolific science fiction writer of all time would have guessed by now that there must be an enormous cover-up? Maybe, but if he knows he's not saying. Perhaps he's afraid that "Foundation" and "Empire" will turn out to be inaccurate. What about Arthur C. Clarke? Surely the most technically accurate of Science Fiction writers with very close ties to NASA would have at least a hint of what's really going on. Again, if so he isn't talking. In a recent Science Fiction survey, Clarke estimates that contact with extraterrestrial intelligent life would not occur before the 21st Century. If the government won't tell us the truth and the major networks won't even give it serious consideration, then what is the big picture, anyway?

Are the EBE's, having conducted a hundred thousand or more abductions (possibly millions worldwide), built an untold number of secret underground bases (Groom Lake, Nevada; Sunspot, Daril, Roswell, and Pine Town, New Mexico, just to name a few) getting ready to return to wherever they came from? Or, from the obvious preparations are we to assume that they are getting ready for a big move? Or is the more sinister and most probable situation that the invasion is essentially complete and it is all over but the screaming? A well planned invasion of Earth for its resources and benefits would not begin with mass landings of ray-gun equipped aliens. A properly planned and executed invasion by a civilization thousands and probably hundreds of thousands of years in advance of us would most likely be complete before even a handful of people (say 12?}realized what was happening. No fuss, no muss. The best ad-vice I can give you is this: Next time you see a flying saucer and are awed by its obvious display of technology and gorgeous lights of pure color—RUN LIKE HELL!

In summary, Mr. Lear contends that our government has for over 40 years been concealing from the public a "horrible truth" concerning an "invasion" of Earth by EBEs (Extraterrestrial Biological Entities). He alleges that the U.S. government has conducted "business with little gray extraterrestrials for about 20 years," i.e. we were "sold" by MJ-12 to the aliens in exchange for technology and to preserve our democracy. He contends that our government agreed to ignore human/cattle abductions and mutilations, but that the deeply sinister purposes of these activities were not completely understood by MJ-12 until about 1984.

Without explaining the EBE's reason(s)to do business with the most powerful nation on Earth when they could covertly continue their activities in the Third World without concern, or why these advanced and powerful aliens would even want or require our "agreement" to continue their activities, Mr. Lear maintains that the purposes of the abductions are: (1)The insertion of a 3mm spherical device through the nasal cavity of the abductee into the brain. The device is used for the biological monitoring, tracking, and control of the abductee. (2) Implementation of Posthypnotic Suggestion to carry out a specific activity during a specific time period, the actuation of which will occur within the next two to five years. (3) Termination of some people so that they could function as living sources for biological material and substances. (4)Termination of individuals who present a threat to the continuation of their activity. (5) Effect genetic engineering experiments. (6) Impregnation of human females and early termination of pregnancies to secure the crossbreed infant.

He cites the history of UFOlogy in the 40's and 5OYs, contending that several crashed saucers and at least three live aliens have been captured and hidden by the government. But would such a powerful adversary permit humans to hold, study and possibly copy crashed saucers or permit us to keep captured aliens, or would they simply take them back?

The EBEs are said to suffer from an atrophied digestive system which requires that they sustain themselves by absorbing through the skin a solution made from certain enzyme/hormonal secretions derived from cattle and humans and collected by ghoulish cattle and human mutilations. The various body parts said to be obtained in this manner are then supposed to be taken for processing to various hidden laboratories jointly maintained by the aliens and CIA in the Southwestern U.S.

Mr. Lear maintains that a 20 year plan for release of UFO information to the public (including the history and intentions of the EBE's) to be completed by 1987-88, was terminated when the "horrible truth" became apparent. Indeed, during the first year of the Carter Administration, various media sources, including Walter Cronkite on the "CBS Evening News" and U.S. News and World Report, reported that before the end of that year the administration was to release UFO information of a "startling" nature. The information was never released. He contends that "Star Wars" is in reality a defensive response to the EBEs, not Soviet nuclear missiles, but does not explain why the EBEs permit us to continue with SDI studies that pose a threat to them.

What follows is a direct transcript between Lear and the National Fringe Sciences Bulletin Board.

Question: You just mentioned that there were 70 other species in contact with this world ...of which 4 others were overt...are they aware of the EBE's?

Lear: Yes they are. The types I will mention are listed in a USAF Academy Physics book called Introductory Space Science Volume 2.B I refer to Chapter 13 about page 8 which lists the ones that are most seen. They are the EBE's, the "blondes" (also called the Nordics). They look just like us but are invariably blond haired and blue eyed. Don't know where they come from but they do not interact with us except for a few abductions now and then.

We also have a species that is similar to us in appearance but they are about seven feet tall and the main difference is that their eyes wrap around the head a little more than ours. Another type listed is a small species about four feet tall, very hairy and extremely strong for their size. We don't know where these guys come from either. All this was in the aforementioned text which was withdrawn by the Air Force in the early 70's from the book. But there are several people who have the original book. The EBE's are about the only ones where we are pretty sure where they come from and that is Zeta Reticuli 1 & 2, a binary star system visible only from the southern hemisphere, spectral class of G2 and 38 light years from here. It is possible that they use some form of the Einstein Rosen Bridge theory (wormholes in space) to get here. We know all this from the work that Marjorie Fish did in the in the early 70's. There is a good article about it in Astronomy Magazine,December, 1974. There was also a reprint of this article in 1976 which had all the comments and rebuttals and rebuttals to rebuttals by Carl Sagan, Bob Schaefer etc. etc.

Question: I remember reading about the characterizations of ET's that you have described about 25 years ago. I also recall a book by a George Adamski, regarding these golden haired aliens. In the Interrupted Journey, I believe it was Betty Hill that under hypnosis revealed many of the invasive techniques used on abductees. Also, perhaps it was in the article on the Zeti Reticuli Incident that a woman under hypnosis reconstructed a 3D model of the Zeta star system with the relative positions of the other stars as they would have appeared as established by computer modeling. I guess one of the primary questions is, if there are other forms visiting and/or interacting with humans, are they completely insensitive to these "arrangements" put out by the EBE's with the government?

Lear: This may be hard to swallow but it's my information from government sources that the blondes adhere to a universal law of non-interference and even though the EBE's are not doing us any favors that they, the blondes will not do anything about it unless the EBE's do something that will affect another part of the universe. Back to Adamski. He has been labeled as a fraud; however, like all things nothing is all black or all white. Some of his stuff was true. But its hard to separate which stuff. He claimed that the blondes came from Venus or Mars which is highly, highly unlikely. As far as the map it was drawn by Betty Hill under hypnosis in 2D. It was Majorie Fish who did the interpretation to bring it into 3D.

Question: I'm curious also as to the government's plans, if any, to deal with an uprising of EBEs should that eventuality occur, or would the technological gap make such an attempt untenable?

Lear: It's my understanding that we have already lost the battle. This is the reason why MJ-12 is in such a panic. They had a lot of well laid plans to inform us, and when the deception was confirmed about 1984 it was all out the window. Back to Betty Hill for a minute...under hypnosis she recalled being given a pregnancy test...a needle was inserted in her stomach. She recalls saying that this was no pregnancy test here on earth (1962).

Amniocentesis was developed around 1972-1973 and uses the exact same procedures. In 1986 a British doctor had given an amniocentesis to a woman and was looking at the fluid under a microscope. He saw a tiny speck and started enlarging it. When he got it big enough to see, what he found was what looked like a computer chip attached to one of the chromosomes. This doctor and six others wrote an open letter in Nature Magazine, one of Britain's most respected scientific journals, along with a picture of the chip, and asked any doctor or scientist anywhere that could held explain what they were seeing.

Question: Recently in the INF treaty negotiations, Gorbachev indicated that despite prior claims, they too were working on an SDI program. Is there any connection between our program and theirs and if the battle is lost, why are these attempts being made?

Lear: I wish I knew the answer to that. Several rumors have come out of the test site recently and one of them was that every test shot this year has been to make a giant room. The shots are very clean and as soon as everything subsides they move in equipment to make walls, ceiling, floors and various levels.

Question: Several critics have highlighted the apparent discrepancies between our medical technology and that of the EBEs as to synthesizing plasma material. Also, technological gaps between our cultures suggest that solicitation of indigenous humans for their undertakings seems akin to asking help from chimpanzees—my analogy—what about these concerns?

Lear: All of these questions are valid and show a lot of thought. All I know is what I wrote. It's very hard to speculate the reasons why or why not a species almost a billion years older than us would do anything. This is not a cop-out...I just don't know and don't want to guess.

It's my understanding from those "in the know;" (and as late as one week ago) that the situation is "ominous."

The Roswell crash was the first recovered flying saucer crash in the U.S. Bill Moore located 90 material witnesses to the crash. It was near Corona, N.M., and a few months ago I interviewed Mrs. Procter near whose ranch this thing crashed. Four bodies were recovered. There is one person still alive at this moment who helped Mac Brazel drag some of the wreckage to the shed. He and Brazel were approached at that time by (I know its hard to believe but the guy is going to come forward soon) an alien who told them both to keep their mouths shut. He is the last guy alive that was directly connected with that retrieval.

The last guy to die was Major Jesse Marcel, the intelligence officer at Roswell who went out and helped pick up the wreckage. Before he died a few years ago he went public with his account which was that the crash was not a balloon or a radar reflector or an airplane. He didn't state what it was, but said it was not of this earth. I have a transcript of the cassette tape of his memories of picking up the wreckage.

Question: Of course, any information you have will be helpful ...What of yourself, why are you coming forward now, particularly placing the spotlight on yourself ...aren't you concerned that there may be some sort of repercussions from the government regarding the stir this is and will continue to cause?

Lear: Let me say that five years ago. I wouldn't have gotten away with this. But things are so screwed up now that one voice talking to...what 50? 100? people can't make any possible difference. Also if something was going to happen it would have happened a few weeks ago. I wrote Dr. Lew Allen, Director of JPL and MJ-12 member that I was going to do a story on his participation in MJ-12 particularly because JPL employed 8,000 people in the Southern California area. I also enclosed a copy of my hypothesis. Dr. Allen has a reputation of responding to all mail in a very prompt manner. But me? I didn't hear anything. Not even a "John Lear you must be crazy." He wrote a letter to Max Fiebleman of Los Angeles on the

18th of December. Max had sent him a copy of the Hudson Valley video and asked Dr. Allen to look at it. Dr. Allen responded that he had taken a quick glance but did not have the time for anything more and on the basis of what he saw determined that it was a blimp. He also wished Max a Merry Christmas. Now...this is one of the world's greatest scientists? Not interested in that Hudson Valley video tape? Gimme a break.

I would be very surprised if some kind of statement from the government is not forthcoming within the year, more probably within six months possibly much sooner...That's about all I can speculate from the information I am getting,

Ace pilot John Lear at the controls of a test vehicle.

AN AIR FORCE LIEUTENANT'S INSIDE STORY
OF THE GOVERNMENT'S POLICY OF SILENCE

During the early 1950s, there was a stepped up attempt on the part of the aliens to establish contact with a variety of individuals from all walks of life. At this point in our Earth time, the "Nordics or Blonds" seemed to be here in abundant numbers. There is even evidence (see the chapter about the experiences of Dr. Frank Stranges) that one of these human-looking types was under "protective custody" and was being housed at the Pentagon. This, I believe, was the ET who had been sent here in exchange for the military officer who supposedly "disappeared" in this fascinating narrative told by a man about whom very little is known.

Retired Air Force Lieutenant and pilot Mel Noel showed up on the "scene" for a short period and then vanished as mysteriously as he had appeared. For less than a year he made the rounds of UFO conventions on the West Coast and apparently even arranged a clandestine meeting with ace researcher John A. Keel in New York, during which time he told Keel that he was able to arrange for rides on board a UFO for a very "select" group who had been predetermined by the space people themselves. Keel says Noel was well dressed, seemed to have a lot of money—they dined in the best restaurant in Manhattan—and surrounded himself with beautiful women who were very "exotic" looking. Though Keel agreed to go for a ride, Noel never got back in touch with him. Keel felt almost certain that the entire conversation was being monitored, perhaps by CIA types who had planted microphones under his table.

Throughout the years, rumors have been rampant that certain of the early contactees in the UFO/New Age movement were being tailed by specially assigned agents for purposes that can only be guessed at.

In some instances, these shadowy figures actually became part of the entourage of the contactees. Cleverly disguising their true intentions on a number of occasions they actually maneuvered into a position of close trust, becoming the personal aides of those who purported to have communicated with alien beings.

95

AMERICA'S TOP SECRET TREATY WITH ALIEN LIFE FORMS

Being susceptible to a higher than average degree of manipulation, the majority of the UFO contactees had no idea that their day-to-day activities were being closely monitored, and in some cases their experiences were even being "guided" along by conniving hands.

As far as can be determined, only one of the early contactees (the majority, like George Adamski, George Van Tassel, and Buck Nelson, are conveniently no longer with us, so we can't quiz them directly) has publicly admitted that a certain percentage of what reportedly happened to him might have been "prompted" in some part by government agents. In front of hundreds of thousands of shocked television viewers, contactee Howard Menger, author of *From Outer Space To You*, recanted a good portion of his original story, live on the "Long John" Nebel show broadcast over WOR-TV in New York.

Later, Menger released a letter in which he said: " ...I wrote a book (Fact/Fiction 1958) based on an actual experience, which I accidentally stumbled upon in an isolated field to the rear of my property in High Bridge, New Jersey. The photographs I took were sent to a department in the Pentagon. It wasn't long afterward that I was contacted and asked if I would cooperate in an experiment based on what I had inadvertently seen and project into this experience an expanded futuristic view of 'things to come' with their help and information. I suppose they must have figured the only way to obtain my silence and cooperation was to put me on the 'team.' "

Menger confessed that he was used to gauge the public's reaction to alien contact. "At first, I was a little shy and more or less tongue-tied, but after my [first few] lectures, I gained in confidence and with the material and suggestions handed to me, I was able to carry on."

As part of the government's "manipulation" of Menger's contacts, he was handed a specimen that was said to be a potato taken from a base on the far side of the Moon. Menger maintains to this day that the specimen was very strange and did seem unusual. "It was the finest piece of dehydration you have ever seen on Earth to date. There is no dehydration plant that can safely dehydrate a whole specimen.

Having investigated Menger's experiences directly, I know that much of what transpired in the apple orchard behind his home in High Bridge, New Jersey was indeed legitimate. Several witnesses reported being "struck" by beams of light from hovering craft. At least two told of a period of five or six hours of missing time while in the orchard, which they could never account for. Still others said they were "chased through the woods" by spiraling "balls of light." One person found his life so abruptly turned around that he left his wife, moved into a trailer, and began to construct weird sculptures of alien landscapes and futuristic worlds. Surprisingly, he had never been artistically inclined prior to his encounter on

Menger's property.

Years ago, I began to get the impression that Menger was not alone in his being "watched " and "manipulated" by "brain-washed," maverick agents operating outside the Constitution, seemingly under the mental influence of the "dark forces."

I first saw Mel Noel while he was lecturing on the West Coast. One of my government contacts had heard about this retired Air Force Lieutenant who was going around "shooting his fool mouth off," talking about things he shouldn't even have known about, much less be discussing in front of an audience. There was some concern that he might go "too far" with his revelations concerning members of the military who had made contact with aliens, but he was not "neutralized" because it was felt nobody outside of a few hardcore "crackpot members" of some "fringe" UFO groups in California would ever accept his story at face value. At the time my contact would have been correct in his assumptions...but today it's a slightly different story, so we'll let Mel Noel defend himself. The following is a transcript of what Noel had to say in front of a huge crowd at the Giant Rock UFO Convention held in the desert in Twenty Nine Palms, California.

His whereabouts are unknown to me today.

PUBLIC LECTURE
BY
MR. MEL NOEL

This all started in 1953 and in the earlier part of 1954. In 1953 we had just come out of the Korean War. None of us were involved in the Korean War, it ended while we were in flight school. We were assigned to a reserve squadron in the western part of the United States, we were what we might best call "line pilots." You have so many duties to perform, you had to fly so many hours a year, so much of it was gunnery, so much was cross country, so much instrument time and aerobatics and such.

We hadn't been with the squadron very long when we were taken apart, three of us, myself, a Lt._____, a Lt._____, and we were notified that we were being released from our duties as line pilots. We were being placed on operation, called "operation units." They told us at the time it was a security matter, and they then took us into the briefing of it. We don't to this day know why we were selected for it. I don't know whether they just took the roster and threw darts at it on the wall or whether they picked it for other reasons, but we had been picked.

They began by explaining the nature of the operation as to the fact that it concerned the UFO, the flying saucers as is better known. They explained to us that if and when anything happened concerning them, as far as relating it, discussing it with friends, relatives, even fellow-officers, the statement to us was, don't even talk to yourself about it. You put it down on the report and take it out of your head and that's where it ends.

They briefed us with several hours of motion picture films that were taken, had been taken by government military aircraft. They showed us many hundreds of still photographs, some were taken by the government, many of which I understand were confiscated from civilians. We were instructed for a number of hours on specific aerial maneuvers, weave patterns, formation flying, the operation of the cameras. We were instructed, we were notified that all the armament, the weapon system, the fire system had been removed from the aircraft.

The aircraft were what was known as F-86A Sabre Jets. Their standard system, standard firing system is six 50-caliber machine guns. These had been all removed and replaced with cameras, gun cameras. Some of these cameras we were informed, contained standard film. The others contained infra-red film. If you're not familiar with infra-red film, the infra-red film will take a picture of something that you cannot see. In other words, you can be vectored into an area on a target that you cannot see by radar and take pictures of objects. You won't see them then, they only come out after the film is developed.

After all the briefing, we discussed it briefly. We had been turned over to a Colonel who was not with the squadron. He was assigned to the operation out of Washington, D.C. We were to respond only to him, have nothing to do any longer with the squadron. He was our flight leader through our entire experience and later on became a very close friend. At the time, however, he was as military as you can find somebody. Everything was strict order. He wanted to discuss nothing else, personal, social or topics of the time in any other way, shape or form. It was all business.

The three of us, and I discussed, prior to the experiences, our common opinion was, that nothing was going to happen. We were aware of the position of the Air Force on it—that there were many reports, that the Air Force made claim to have investigated these things, and we figured that we were in essence the dumb dumbs, that we were going through the paces to live up to these statements. In other words, we were to investigate these things. This was it! But we really didn't expect to see anything, let alone hear anything.

The first few missions were, we might say, the orientation runs. We were closing up our formation flying under different conditions. We were operating at approximately 38,000 feet altitude, six or seven miles above the surface of the earth, and we were operating over the Rocky Mountains of Idaho, Utah and on up north. The first week produced the first sighting. We had been instructed in formation flying. If you can imagine, we flew in what is called a diamond formation.

If you can picture a baseball diamond. Second base is the flight leader. Third base is left wing man. First base is the right wing man. Home plate is called slot position. I drew the slot position; I didn't like it, but that's what I got. The operation was to maintain this formation, this diamond formation. Upon a sighting the formation was closed in, 60 feet was from wing tip to wing tip. We were drilled until this became measurable almost to the inch. As soon as a sighting was made, a visual contact, there was an order change; we broke into a weave pattern. Now the weave pattern operated this way. As soon as the formation broke, second base and third base broke starboard, that means broke right, and home plate and first base broke left onto the target. If the target were dead ahead, it was projectory all ahead. If it were left, it would be home base and first base that would have first projectory. If it were on the right, third base and second base would have first projectory.

As it happened, the sightings were all to our left, and the first one to see them was _____. He always saw them first; I don't know why. It wasn't what he said, but how he said it I think, that got to all of us real quick. His statement was, "Bogies, nine o'clock level." Bogey is just Air Force slang. It just means foreign aircraft, something you don't know what it is, something that doesn't belong to us, and we were convinced of that. There were 16 of them, and they were operating in a vertical V formation. They were strung out seven and nine, seven aloft and nine going aft.

They were operating at approximately the same speed. They maintained right alongside of us. We were operating 680 knots. That was surface speed. Military Jets, there are two speeds, two air speeds; you have surface and military speeds. Surface is a cruising speed as it is better known in civilian aircraft, and military is everything that can be put into the boiler, the after-burner. You can get up into over 700 miles an hour, We could not obtain Mach one or speed of sound in level flight, but we could obtain it in a dive. We very seldom did it because of the vibration incurred, so we were maintaining our surface speed, and they were maintaining at the same speed and the same altitude as we were.

At this speed their appearance was a relatively distinct physical outline with a best described "aura" surrounding them. I think perhaps the best way of relating this aura is, if you have ever seen a street light or a neon sign in a fog, in the rain, they seem to be very fuzzy, and this is the type of appearance it gives.

The effect upon myself—I was pretty excited! I didn't know what was happening. I had never seen one of these things before, let alone 16 of them. And a thousand questions raced through your mind, and as fast as these questions came, you're moving. The weave was called and off we went, and were closing on them, and we were given very distinct closing minimum distances. In other words, you don't get too close. We already knew what had happened to aircraft that had gotten too close, and we didn't want to go through that.

We, to the best of my knowledge, did not get any, very few if any, photographs, pictures, the first time. The reason being was that the cameras had been hooked up with the automatic gunsight system. This automatic gunsight is a little electronic wonder which pins the target, holds the target, goes through a series of electronic manipulations and aims the guns and fires them. This all takes 20 some odd seconds under standard conditions, and it wasn't enough, it wasn't fast enough; it had taken too long. I think the cameras triggered several times, but it was too late. We had to back off on the opposite leg by that time.

If you can picture this weave, we would break when we are in our formation; this is the slot and right wing man breaking toward left. We are now closing on a target, a common target. We are closing projectory. In other words, if we were to go to target, we would collide ourselves, so as we would reach approximately 100 feet wingtip to wingtip, the wide man would go low, he would go under and the near man would come over and reverse position, and we would then reverse and come back 90 degrees on our next leg back. In the meantime, the other two men had reversed their leg, and were now heading on target.

The effect or purpose of this, was to have two aircraft on the same target at all times. In other words, confirming evidence, opinion of pilot as well as camera. Whatever was produced, there were two people looking at the same thing at the same time. At the same time when you reversed your leg, you were blind. You couldn't see it, but the other two pilots were covering you at all times. If anything were happening, they would notify you.

Our weave pattern didn't go on very long because they broke their formation into four groups of four. This answered a question. We thought perhaps they were centrally controlled by one unit and they were locked on and controlled, however it was, we didn't know how they were propelled, and they split into four groups of four, and then after a minute or so, they split individually, and they demonstrated some things that by the book can't happen. And it's like the bumble bee, he can't fly—that's by the book, but he doesn't know that, so he goes ahead and does it. These things were doing things that you couldn't do in the air according to the book. It was impossible for a human being if there were human beings in them, we didn't know then, to survive the breaking from what we were estimating their top speed at approximately 3,000 miles an hour, to a dead stop, and I mean instantly! Just as fast as when you turn the switch off the lights go off, that's as fast as they stopped, and they accelerated just about as fast. When they turn the juice on, they are going. As they would accelerate, when they would stop, the physical outline was very clear.

They were approximately 150 to 180 feet in diameter and about 20 or 30 feet thick at the widest midsection, cross section. One point that we didn't agree on was whether the center section was approximately 30 or 40 feet in the center of the saucer elevated, raised out when they would stop. It was so difficult; they would operate so fast, and our observation was at times so limited, it was difficult to tell whether the center section was raised all the time or whether it just elevated when they would stop for observation. As they would accelerate, the haze around them, the aura would change color just like the spectrum. In other words, if you were to go over the spectrum, they would advance through those various stages. There was no evidence of sound, we of course being seated in, we couldn't smell anything; we couldn't feel anything. Other than slight compass malfunction, we did not have any instrument malfunction. All systems operated normally. The compass malfunction is not unusual anyway. You get this in many areas, and we didn't experience any ill and uncomfortable effects ourselves, other than what we would have put in our own minds.

The entire experience lasted about eight minutes and as quickly as they appeared, we didn't see them coming, but as quickly as they appeared, they were gone. I mean when they go, they go. They strung off just like a string of beads, and you could count them out of sight. We were pretty excited about the entire thing! This certainly was something new. We didn't know what to think of it. As far as we knew, we were safe. Everything was going along fine. When we landed, we were reminded of the security. We were given reports; we filled the reports out. Whether we got any films or not, we don't know, they pulled the cans as fast as we landed and we never did see them; we didn't even know where they went.

The security was constantly pointed out to us. It was reminded to us exactly, not what would happen if, but we had an example of this, not during our experience, I shouldn't say this, but it was right around the same time. One of the line pilots, he was not on this assignment, just in his regular line of duties, had seen a few of them. And he decided that he was going to tell more than just a few people about it, so he sold to Fawcett Publications what he saw, and he received $500.00 for his efforts, and within 24 hours after he had signed the contract with them, the article hadn't had a chance to appear of course, within 24 hours after he signed the contract, he was in the Aleutian Islands, he was reassigned. Now at that time, it was commonly known as a suicide assignment, it's a one way ticket. It's one you get that you don't come back from. So, of course, this weighed over us. We thought a great deal about talking about this to anybody.

Many, many questions occurred to us. We would discuss these for many hours alone, just the three of us, cause the Colonel wouldn't talk to us about it. We didn't know whether it was just happening to him or what was going on at that point.

We flew a number of missions between the sightings without anything happening, and it was just like any other run. The second time was just a few days later, and this time there were only five of them. _____ spotted them again. In the meantime we had, by our recommendation, they had changed the triggering of the cameras from the automatic to the manual. In other words, the stick buttons, which meant that we could fire or just shoot as many frames as we possibly could at any time, and I'm certain that we obtained a number of photographs this way. I remember now, our calculations of aiming were up to us, up to our eyes rather than by electronic calculations. If given the proper amount of time, the gunsight would have done a much better job, but in case of expediency here, we didn't have enough time, so they had converted it.

The second experience was just like the first, as far as what we were seeing. We didn't know if they were the same ones or not, but there they were, there were just five of them! They moved about, up and down, in vertical oscillation, down this way. When they would turn or change direction, there was no bank, they were unaffected it would seem by the various laws that had been drilled into us for months and months in flight school; the laws of lift and drag, yaw and gravity. The forces of stopping or acceleration didn't seem to affect anything or anybody, that we knew. We felt we were getting used to it, and yet something was going on inside of us that we hadn't begun to understand. It was all very exciting!

When something is exciting, you're only focusing upon what is happening, not on what it means. This was brought home, I think, very seriously on the third sighting. When it was made, there were five again, this was just a couple of days later. When called, we were looking, and he notified us that they were there, at the time we assumed things, and you shouldn't do that, we assumed the change of position of weave and in close formation, 60 ft. tip to tip, you haven't got much room for mistakes and there was a little jockeying there, because the call never came. He didn't call a change, and after less than a minute, we had a change of radio channel. This was given to us in a code which is called an inverted alphabetical code. If you take WXYZ and invert that numerically, it would be 1-2-3-4. This is the way the codes were changed or the radio channels were changed, through this alphabetical system. We were given the letters—it took me probably 20 to 25 seconds to convert it, convert the letters and figure the numerical values and then to spin it in, And what I did, I didn't know of course, in that short span of time, you're not wondering why you're doing something, you're just doing it, and this is just part of your orientation.

You go through quite a bit of, a moment of truth searching during something like this. You wonder why it's happening to you. You wonder what you're doing here, what this is all about. It starts coming at you and you don't have time to think about it. We thought we were getting used to seeing these things. We could live with them! But the experience of the communication was something that we weren't really ready for, and we didn't expect it and couldn't understand what this was all about.

When I hit the channel, there was a voice speaking on it and it was not me; it wasn't either of the group, anyone of the flight, or the other three. And the voice was answering questions as such. Now, at no time did I ask any questions. And no time did any of the other three pilots ask any questions, uttered them verbally, and yet we were hearing something that was coming through, just like we were listening to or talking to each other or to a tower on the ground. It was very clear. The enunciation, pronunciation, vocabulary, was excellent. The rate of speech was very slow. We were told later on by the flight leader, by the Colonel, that he had been asking the questions.

He said, "I did not say any of them." He said, "I was merely thinking them."

He said, "They did not answer all of them, just a few." The first statement that had been made, and we had to at this time remember, more or less read in what the question might be, which he later on told us. He said the first question was, "Do you believe in God?" Now, he aid, "the reason I asked them this was, if there was somebody there and they did, and if they did, then the odds were with us that they weren't hostile." And the answer, the statement was that we heard was, "We believe in the Almighty Power of the Universe. You must understand that there are over 150 billion universes, and that there are many forms and orders of Gods in each and every one of them."

I am not relating to you verbatim. After 12 years, I can't remember exactly word for word, but this is very very close to the exact wording of what was said. Something like this doesn't leave you as such. The next statement was referring to the existence of life here, where they came from, what they believed in. They said that, ah, the question had to be–he said the question was—do you—I am trying to think of what excited the question, exactly how the question was worded, because the statement was in effect—The existence of Noah in the Bible, the authenticity of it as such, they referred to it as an erroneous history book. They said for instance, "Noah's Ark was never a boat. It was an arc of time or a period of time, which this man was a Ruler, and he ruled over a civilization, and he said if we went back and investigated the Latin, we would find Noah meant Inca, and the Incas were the last of the Noah civilization."

And they referred to, they made the statement that our scientists had made statements based upon theories that life cannot and therefore does not exist on the other planets in this system, and they said that they were confirming those statements. He said, "Life does not and cannot exist on these other planets; it's all inside the planets, it's all in the interior, just as the house of the Lord, This is the house of the Lord we live in, the interior of the planet, and they stated that life originated here the same way, on the interior of the planet. And he said that it still exists that way."

The next question must have been as to exactly who are you, where are you from? Because the statement was, "Our crews are made up of individuals from planets known to you as Venus, Jupiter, Mercury, Mars and Saturn," and they referred to Saturn as the head "Tribunal Planet." In other words, the leaders of the state met here to discuss the affairs of state. They went into a number of other things that may or may not be important; by discussion with legal advice, much of this, I can only discuss about 10 per cent of what took place.

The total effect of the experience on us was when we landed, we couldn't walk! We were crawling! We were on our hands and knees, and we weren't ready for it. All we wanted was out, and this is what we told them then. They gave us sedation; we told them we said, we want out of this, we don't want any more to do with it, anyway we can get out of it. Whether it was his efforts or not, we were relieved of the assignment the next day. One thing that was out of order was that as soon as we landed, he insisted, he dictated to us and he said, "You do not report the communication." He said, "Everything else, but do not report the communication." This is unusual. We didn't care to report anything.

It was a relief to get away from it and back to the regular duties. The problem was now, how do you live with it? I talked to veterans of combat and seen some of the psychological effect of first hand combat. I don't know if any of you here have seen combat. I have not. I hope you haven't from what I have seen, the effect of it upon others; it's a brutal thing. And yet, some of this is similar to it. You weigh mankind. You weigh your own and you weigh the thinking of the world, and you say where does this fit, where does this fit in my thinking, in my way of life? Well, I have no time for it. I haven't got the answers. I don't know where to go to get the answers, so I'm going to pass. I'm just going to go ahead just like everybody else. There's a couple hundred million living, having, having a good time, and I can do the same thing, I can do without this, and it's not easy to do without it. Not that you want it, something happened to you. You were involved whether you wanted it or not, and here you are now, what are you going to do with it?

This was just the first part of it, because the real testing was coming into being. For about two months after we were off the assignment, we began to figure that we could live with this thing. The three of us, the other two pilots and I talked about it quite a bit, and we decided that we couldn't help each other very much. The answers weren't here. It was just opinion against opinion. We could only confirm what all of us had seen and heard, so where do you go from here? The Colonel wouldn't talk to us. About two months later he called me up and he said, "Come on over, I want to talk to you." And I said boy maybe this is it, maybe these are the answers.

When I got over there, —and had already gotten there, the Colonel was very nervous. He was pacing up and down, and he said, "I've got to talk to somebody." He said, "I've got to let you know what's happening." And we just sat there with bated breath as to well let's have it! He said, "I've got to make a decision; I'll do that myself." He said, "I just want to associate myself with somebody who can understand," and he said, "I think you fellows are the only ones with whom I can do it."

He said, "I've found the truth," and then he made a statement which I think he was making for his own benefit as well as ours. He said, "I am an Officer in this Government, in this Armed Forces, in the United States Air Force, and I have a duty, a responsibility and an image to maintain," and he said, "The truth doesn't agree with it." He said, "I've got to go one way or the other." He said, "I can't live with both." He said, "I don't know what they do with what's happening, but it's not getting out," and he said, "That's all." And it was. He wasn't going to discuss anything else. He said, "I'll see you later," and bid us good night.

So what we thought was going to happen, didn't happen at all, except we didn't realize that he had opened the door. We were in for almost about ten minutes of experiences of his that he related to us concerning these things. And it was several weeks later before he called again. This time he called, he said, "Come on over," and he said, "I'm going to let you in on it." We went over; I got there and other fellows came in.

We sat down and he told us that this wasn't new to him by any means, he had been on this for quite a while. He said, "The communication wasn't the first time. It was the first time anybody else was along when he had communication. He said that he had innumerable experiences with them. He felt that his experience was invaluable as far as the procedures of the Government, of the Air Force now in tracking and pursuing them because of it." And then he started to relate some of the experiences to us.

It seemed by his statements that the experiences were always three or four months old, they hadn't just happened, and most of them varied little except for the time and the place, the weather conditions, the speeds and the shapes of the objects. He explained to us that saucers were incapable of flying from planet to planet. He said, "They can't do this because they operated in the electronic-electrical fields surrounding the planets." He compared this to a current of electricity in a piece of wire. In other words, if you take a piece of wire, and you conduct electrical current: through that wire by resistance—now by inverting that theory, we pass the wire through the field and control the speed by resistance once again. I guess it doesn't work quite that easy, but this is how he compared it. This is how they operate.

"Even though the electrical fields overlap between planets," he said, "they are not strong enough at the outer distances so these saucers are carried by mother ships." He said, "The mother ships were up to ten miles long and they would carry as many as 300 saucers. They had several thousands of crews and he said, they all come from different planets, and he said, they even come from planets outside this galaxy. "

He said, "It only took a few minutes to go from here to another planet, because the mother ship was capable of the speed of light at which time it becomes infinity, that there is no time passage as such, as we know it here."

The one experience that he related to us which I think was outstanding was the contact he had with them ...when he spoke with the, he saw them, and he related this to us the very next day after it happened. He called me up and he was very excited! He said, "Get over here fast!" and I did. He said, "I've seen them; I drove with them to where the saucer is. I talked with them. I talked with a guy called a Master! He has the most fantastic mind that I ever talked to." And we said, "Well, settle down Pete. Let's hear it."

He said that he had had a cross-country the night before, he was flying to Luke Air Force Base, that's out in Phoenix, Arizona, He said that on the way down, it was uneventful, nothing had taken place. He said it this way. "I don't know what you think about dreams." He said, "Now don't get me wrong, I wasn't asleep." He said, "I was wide awake." He said, "I had a daydream or a sequence thing or whatever you want to call it, but I had a little sequence thing in which I imagined or dreamed that after I had gotten landed on the field and went into operations, they told me that they have reserved a staff car for men (and this is not unusual for a man of his rank), and they told him that they had reserved a motel room for him (and that's not unusual). He said that "..after he got to the motel, the room clerk told him the number of the room, and he said that at 7:30 that night there was a knock on the door and he said that there were two men there at the door that he had never seen before." He said, "That's where it ended, that's as much as I had received as such." He said, "That's all I knew about it."

"Well, he said, that when he got down there and he went into operations, they told him they had reserved a staff car for him." He said, "I passed that off as just a coincidence." And he said, "they told me they reserved a motel room for me." He said, "even though it was the same name of the motel, I passed that off as just a coincidence. There are just so many motels there at that time." He said, "But when I got to the motel and the room number coincided, he said, I started getting upset." He said, "I figure that three out of three was going pretty strong, and he said, "I took a hot bath and I tried to settle down; I laid down, I tried to read." And he said, "After awhile, I couldn't get my eyes off that clock and at 7:30 there was a knock on the door." And he said, "I didn't know whether to go to the door or out the window." He said, "I figured I had been through an awful lot and maybe this was it; this was too much!"

He said, "I knew I was perhaps reading into it and I went to the door, I opened the door, and there were two young fellows standing there about college age. They had suits on and hats, and he said the only unusual thing about them was their eyes." He said, "Their eyes looked as if they could look right through you," And he said, "The one fellow, they addressed him by his name and rank, and they introduced themselves and they said their names were Mike and Dave for all practical purposes." And he said, "The fellow who was speaking, called himself Mike; he extended his hand," and he said, "I extended mine, and I shook hands with him." He said, "The only definition I can use was a feeling that went through me when I did it." He said, "It was love. That's all I know." He said, "I never experienced anything like that before between man and woman in my life. That's just what it was. I put my life in his hands at that moment," he said, "If he would have told me to jump off the Empire State Building, I would have done it and I wouldn't have been hurt." He said, "I didn't know what I was in for, but I no longer feared anything."

He said, "We went outside; we got in a car, a Chevy car. We drove outside of Phoenix. They informed me that they were taking me aboard a saucer, and they were going to allow me an audience with a man they called the Master." And he said, "That they told him that a Master was the highest physical form, that this was the highest form physically in intelligence, and then after that an individual becomes a Godfather." And they said, "That he had performed well in his duties, and this is why he was being allowed this audience." They said, "It would take approximately a half hour so that he could prepare any questions that he wanted to ask." And he said, "He was trying to focus, trying to be objective about it." So he said, "That it as pretty, pretty exciting!"

He said, "They got out, I figured about 18 miles outside the city and they left the main highway and they drove off a little road into the desert. And after awhile, in that area the property of the land was very rocky, very hilly and it was growing dusk, he said, and they turned the headlights on the car, and then they drove off the road." He said, "After a while they came over a bluff, the car stopped; they hadn't turned the switch off though, or the lights off though, but the lights and the engine stopped and he said he could look out and see the bottom of a valley, so to speak, there." He said, "There was a saucer sitting there on a tripod, on three legs." He said, "It was about 150 feet in diameter." He said, "It was just sitting there, that's all."

He said, "They got out of the car and when they did, these two fellows took their suits and hats off and their shirts, and they had a one piece jump-type of suit on underneath." He said, "This was one piece including the shoes and that they wore a belt, and the belt had a metal disk in it, in the center of it." He said, "They produced one of these metallic discs for him and they told him to hold it between the palms of his hands." He showed it to us, like this. And he had the disk, he still had the disk, he showed it to us. And they said, "To hold it in the palms of his hands and hold it to his stomach, and this would guarantee no ill effects when passing through the force fields as he entered the saucer."

He said, "They walked until they were about 80 feet from the saucer and stopped and they just stood there." And he said, "I started to talk, and they just looked at me; that was enough to say, just be quiet for now." And he said, "After a moment, there was a sort of a ramp that came down from the saucer and a man came down out of it." And he said, "The fellow stood out there." He said, "Although there was no verbal uttering going on, it was fairly obvious that they were discussing things, that they were talking things over, and they then turned to him and said, it's alright, everything is okay, we can go aboard." And he said, "They walked to the ship, he said, the man who had come outside had already gone back in; they all walked in there."

He said, "The entire place glowed like a, in other words, there was no concentration of light as we have it here, we see it in these bulbs. The ceilings, the floors, and the walls, they all glowed equally." He said, "They took me first to the control section, the center of it." He described it to us. He said, "They described it fairly well to him exactly how the thing operates; their speeds, their controls." He said, "They had many control systems that were similar to ours already, their use of television and radar as such. They had these systems also."

He said, "They also told him about scout ships, they were unmanned, they were merely instrument packages; these things were just four to six feet in diameter. They could send these out and control them, radio control them and put them into an area where they would be undetected where a larger craft would be spotted. They said they could send these in and relay information back." In other words, they would send back a telecast just as we would from a telestation and produce it on a screen there in the saucer and they could see it.

He said, "They took him into an outer room then and informed him that it was about time for his audience, and he said he walked into this room, and he said, it was always difficult when you changed rooms to tell whether the lights just went on or they were already on, he said, but it seemed to be always new brilliance and the lights were particularly strong but not uncomfortable,"

He said, "He sat down on a bench affair on the outside, he said he could tell they were on the outer perimeter because the roof slanted, and he said they sat there for a few minutes."

"After a few minutes, two women came into the room, and he said that by the way you fellows think as well as myself, well, I'm just a red-blooded American boy and he said, they were pretty groovy chicks." And he said, "They were real beautiful women, so he said, you know after all, I'm progressive and he said, I just came into my natural way of thinking!" He said, "They started laughing and giggling and I all of a sudden realized that they knew what I was thinking."

He said, "I was very embarrassed." He said, "I went to get a cigarette and I noticed I hadn't seen anybody smoking or even facilities for such, and they explained that it was just a nasty habit I had here and that I would get rid of it sooner or later. And they asked him if he was thirsty and he said he could have drank the Red Sea dry about then." And he said, "They went out and brought back a glass of what he closely compared to as grape juice; he said it wasn't unusual." He said, "After I said yes, I'm thirsty, all of a sudden I realized maybe they were going to give me a glass of Bardahl, or a glass of Rye, and maybe I wasn't ready for this, but he said it wasn't unpleasant at all,"

And he said that when they went out of the room to bring him back this glass of whatever it was, he said, the one fellow turned to him and he said, "How old do you think the young ladies are?" He said, "Maybe you would be interested to know that the one is 78 years old, and the other one is 146." And he said, "You know, that's the first time I ever thought of making love to a 146 year old woman."

He said the ladies hadn't come back the second time, but two other men came into the room and this Master came in. And he said it was obvious that the Master was a senior person by his dress. He said, "They all wore these one-piece jumpsuit outfits, but he said, they also had these little colored patches on their suits. He said that one of the men explained that this established their degree of intelligence, in other words, the rank of intelligence. He said the Master was introduced to him, was told that this Master was from Venus, and he sat down."

The Master told him, "You may ask me any question you want, but I won't necessarily answer any of them." He said, "Of course I went into high gear again with my questions as to what I felt most important, so I started repeating the questions that we had in our communications, and he said the answers were almost the same." In other words, "Do you believe in God?" "Yes, to the Almighty Power of the Universe." He said, "There are many degrees and forms of Gods and many spiritual aethers, he said, they go on and on and on." And he said, "But as it is related to that fine little history book called the Bible that you have," he said, "As God is, man may become." He said, "That this is so, you will become. We all go through the same."

And he said that he asked him what was happening, what was taking place, why they were coming, what was going to be taking place in the future. And he said, that, "We think of it here that they are responsible for the planet as long as it has been here." He said, "They are assigned positions of responsibility in which they have control or are responsible for so many hundreds of millions of spirits." He said, "Reincarnation was a problem because it was difficult to send so many people back. He explained they had assumed certain important responsibilities as to the conditions of this planet, and he said that things weren't too good here." Heck, we already knew that! And he said that, "This was more as a clearing house and that they sent their problem makers over here for a while." I guess we got them all!

He predicted a number of things. He made statements pertaining to the future. Now at this time, this was in 1954, these predictions were interesting, fascinating to hear, but relatively, personally, they weren't that important. He made certain remarks concerning California.

He stated, "That a change of cycle was coming about. He said the earth went through cycles of so many thousands of years and as one cycle closed out, the next one started." It wasn't any abrupt action like flipping a switch, now it's day, now it's night, but one ebbed out, the other came in. He said the coming of the new one had already started or was about to start at that time it seems, and that the new one would not be in full swing until around the year 2000."

He said, "That there would have to be many geographical changes made in preparation for this, there will have to be many changes in other systems." He said, "As a result of this, there would be many religious upheavals, political upheavals and so on, that will be of natural consequence, because the political leaders won't have the answers for these things. They can only answer so many things that happen, but beyond that, it's a miracle or an act of God, but all of a sudden God is here."

He referred to Christ as Christ Jesus, and he said that, "He was a Son of God, but not the Son of God." In other words, "There were many, many millions of Sons of God of different degrees. He was just a higher degree of intelligence of a Son of God when he visited here." He said, "In this day and age he would be called nothing more than a clairvoyant being and that's all." He said, that, "Most of your predictions of the miracles in the Bible are built up out of proportion." He said, "You can actually assimilate the realization of them if you were to, so to speak, gear them back down. That it is possible and they are happening around you every day. You just don't label them as a miracle and write them off the book."

He said, "Out of the entire thing, there would be much holocaust." He said, "At one time, it was possible for the civilization to save itself." He said, "The people of the earth produce vibrations, and these are positive and negative vibrations and there are vibrations of love and, as we know, there are many forms of love. He said that the vibrations were, however, overwhelmingly so negative. The world was overwhelmingly materialistic and they were no longer objective to things which they could not see. They would rather have something they can hold on to." We will find out of course, ourselves, we don't possess anything, nothing, not even our children.

I think it's how we use it as well as ourselves, we're sort of licensed to operate ourselves here. I'm not sure which department issues this license, but we have the use of the land, we have the use of the air, the use of the water, it would seem. There is no tax to be paid on this, except to the, shall we say, the Universal Law of Cause and Effect. And he went into some degree in this, explaining what we have come to know now as a Karmic pattern. This is an old law of the Far East.

He said he defined reincarnation more specifically. He said, "They went through voluntarily, reincarnation." He said, "However, we are not quite at that level of consciousness here. That most people won't even accept it, let alone know how to utilize it or how to utilize their past lives."

He said, "Reincarnation is just as simple as grade school." He said, "You go to first grade; you study the subject matter, and at the end of the year you take the examination, and one of three things happen. Number one—you pass, and you go on to the next grade, the next higher step and higher opportunity. Number two—

you fail the test, and you take the grade over." In other words, you come back; you get another vehicle, another body; you go through it again, second chance. "Number three—you fail the test or you fail earlier in the schedule and you drop out, and you drop out and you float around for hundreds, maybe thousands of years before coming into a state of awareness that you can come back and eventually you do come back."

"If you examine your child prodigies and the intellects of your different people, he said, you will find that number one, you will find many of the answers there." And he said, "You will also find that a child upon close investigation, until they are about three or four years old, has vivid recollection of their past lives." He said, "It won't take much investigation for you to find this out." "Study your own children, he said, many of the little stories they are telling aren't stories, it has already happened to them."

He went into diet. He said, "They were vegetarians. They do nor consume meat because the animals contain spirit bodies just as we do; contain the spirit." He said, "We do not believe in destroying the vehicle of the spirit or altering their Karmic pattern." He said that, "They do not believe in inebriation." He did not say, we don't drink, he didn't say they didn't drink, he said, "They do not believe in intoxicating the body," that's how they worded it.

The predictions he stated at that time; they discussed Cuba. He said, "An island close to the southeast of the United States would be taken over by the 'Bear.' " He said he always referred to them as the Great Bear, the Russians." And he said that, "A major conflict would arise out of a seemingly insignificant war or insignificant conflict in the southeastern part of Asia," which we might call Vietnam. He aid, "This would seemingly be very small and insignificant, but it would advance to the state which could be a major war between the three major powers in which he said, the Great Bear would join with the Americans against the Orientals."

Now, remember back in 1954, about the biggest threat that China had on winning a war was throwing rice, and now they have nuclear power. This to me is not nearly the threat that germ warfare is. It's true, they still don't have an air force, they don't have a navy; they don't need it. All they need is a couple of submarines and get close enough and you got an epidemic. We can bring it on our-selves! We still import some things from China. We can import the entire death and destruction of this country. You know how big a germ is? People say, "What's a flu epidemic?" That's just as fast as it spreads, it goes pretty fast, doesn't it?Germ warfare can wipe out a nation just as fast; not sick! Dead! You say, so what! You're coming back anyway!

The overture of this entire thing, the seeking and then the why, what to do, where do we go from here? He stated that, "This Master told him that out of the entire holocaust, 7,000,000 people would survive." Do you know what 7,000,000 is in the population of the planet? It's a drop in the bucket, very few! He said, "How will they survive?" He said, "They will be the ones who will find their own salvation." He said, "They will heed the warnings." He said, "What do you mean by warnings?"

Well, he had made a prediction. He stated that, "There would be a major land change in Southern California, he said, but there would be two warning signs. He said 90 days before this, the volcanoes of Mt. Pelee or Mt. Vesuvius would erupt," He said, "When this happens, for those who heed it, he said, they will move; for those who don't, they will find Southern California inundated under the waters of the Pacific Ocean." He said, "These waters will extend as far inland and north as far as Salt Lake City, Utah." That's an awful lot of land, that's a lot of people. That takes care of seven million right there; I don't know how many more.

He said, "There would be major land changes, geographical changes all over the planet in preparation." It was of interest to me, I see a gentleman friend of mine seated in the back there, who showed me an article a few weeks ago, a little article which stated, relating how an island emerged out of the Pacific Ocean off the coast of Chile, witnessed by many people. It's still there, it didn't go back down, it's still there; an island 60 miles long!

In some other predictions or prophecies that he made, it is stated that before the continent of Japan, the greater part of the Pacific Ocean will emerge from the Pacific. There will be the emergence of land mass in the southern Pacific. When an island comes up out of the Pacific, that's land mass.

There are many ways you can interpret or misinterpret many things. It's very difficult to be objective at times, to be realistic. And you say, first, we want the facts, then what do we do with them. He said, "It's too late for the planet as a whole." He said, "By the time your children are four or five years old they are so thoroughly indoctrinated to prejudice, hatred, distrust, selfishness, he said, you block the doors to them." He said, "There is your only hope." He said, "We begin to educate our children when they are three months old. By the time they are fifteen years of age, they have mastered telepathy. "

The Colonel never did this, he never dictated to us. He never said at any time, this is so, this is the way it will be, this is what you have to do; he never said that. He said, "Here it is. Do what you want with it. Take it or leave it."

We were separated shortly thereafter, and I went back to Connecticut, to my home state. And I had given him the address of my parents back there, and I went into business in Connecticut. And for two years I thought, awe, just bury it, just bury it, don't think about it, A number of little things happen and the subject comes up and you can't talk about it, so you don't, and you sit there and say, well gee, I wonder what it would be worth if they knew what I knew, if it would help them any. You say, well, I better not. So you just sit there and listen to them talk about it.

In September, my mother called me at the office. She said, "You got a telegram here from Colonel so and so." I said, "Well, open it, read it to me," so she did, and he was at the Westchester County Airport in White Plains, New York. There was a phone number there, and I called him. He says, "Come on down. Let's get together." He sounded very happy. So I did. I went right down and saw him, and he was very happy. He was probably the happiest man I had ever seen, and we went over old times for a few minutes.

And I said, "What's happening Pete?" He said, "I made it! I made the grade! I'm going on!" I said, "Oh, did you get a promotion?" And he said, "No, I'm going with them." And I said, "Boy," I said, "It's been awhile, let me sit down for this. What do you mean by going with them?! He says, "I'm going with them, just the way it sounds." And I said, "How much time do you have?! And he said, "About 30 days, within 30 days I'm going," Well, we talked about other things, and he came up to the house a couple of times.

If he wasn't at the base, I called the base every day from then on, twice a day, sometimes three times a day. Sometimes I called he wouldn't be there of course, so I would leave a message and he'd call me back. And it's like waiting for a baby, except in reverse, you're waiting for someone to leave. You're happy about it, you wonder! I told him, "You don't seem to be upset about this. You don't have any fear." He said, "No, I'm probably one of the happiest men you'll ever know." He said, "I'm looking forward to this like a kid to Christmas." He said, "I'm going and I know it!" He said, "It's a terrific feeling, let me tell you." He said, "But I know where I'm going, I guess that helps." I said, "Do you really, do you really know where you're going?" He said, "Wherever it is, it's right, and whatever it is, I found it." And he said, "Let me tell you, you keep seeking and you'll find it." He said, "Just don't, don't ever misuse it. Don't ever misinterpret it. Always be objective, never dictate with it, and he said, you'll find the Truth."

On the twenty-seventh day, I called down there and they told me he was out and they took a message to have him call me and he didn't call me back. So I called again, and they said, "No, he was overdue." He was on a mission, he was out over the Atlantic Ocean. And so I waited and called back, and they said, "No, he was reported missing, assumed down." And I said, "Well, have you launched a search?" And they said, "Yes,"And I said, "Is it a major or minor search?" And they said, "Minor search." And I said, "How tong to a major search?" And he said, "We can't tell you that. "

Now a search is a very expensive proposition, man and materials. It may cost $40,000 to search for somebody just in a matter of hours, and they just don't call a major search right away. There are so many hours on a local search, minor search, and then they go into a major search. So I asked him how far the major search was off, and he told me so many minutes. This answered my question in another way, so I said, "Fine." So I called back in the morning, and he said, "No trace, presumed lost," and after so much time of course, the searching time is off; when it's off, it's finished. And I asked him if there was anything, and they said, "No, no trace." To my knowledge, they haven't, they haven't found him, never did.

This, of course, is nothing, nothing original about this. There are some 800 military personnel that disappear every year without report of where they are, where they went. This is in the air, I don't know how many disappear on the ground. I am now associated with a man who resigned his position in Washington just two months ago, who was with this assignment. He was one of the heads of this. To sit and listen to the things that he tells, makes this mild. And he wants to get it out too. It's not easy. It's as I say, not to dictate, just to say, here it is, do with it what you want.

Mel Noel says he communicated with a UFO via radio.

ALIENS HELD PRISONER BY EARTH GOVERNMENTS

Perhaps it is a form of mistaken retaliation by those in the military who believe in the philosophy of an eye for an eye, and a tooth for a tooth.

Maybe, it is seen as a type of "revenge" against the EBEs for taking more and more humans against their will and turning them into zombies, with their minds blanked out of all that they have undergone, but still possessing the scars to prove they were amply "abused" by the grays.

In any regard, several sources have come forward recently to claim that our government is trying to get the "upper hand " and has actually taken several aliens prisoner and are holding them hostage under primitive conditions that can only be called barbaric.

Diane Tessman knows of such matters first hand, as she was herself whisked away at an early age on board a space ship, where she underwent examination, muscle tissue having been taken before she was returned to her parent's farm, only to find that she now shared her mind with an alien who had actually "blended" with her on an operating table inside that craft. Fortunately for the long-haired blonde—who is a former state section director for the Mutual UFO Network, and now heads her own group in Holland—the space beings she is in contact with are among "the good guys" who always surround her with a protective beam of white light whenever they wish to communicate. Many of the messages she receives concern themselves with the betterment of humanity and the fear that we might be poisoning our globe, and should do something constructive about the situation before it becomes too late and we kill ourselves off in an ecological disaster of an undreamed of magnitude.

Recently, Diane's "sources"'—some with government affiliations—have alerted her to the fact that several aliens are now being held against their will in several locations. What makes the matter of extra concern is that these aliens are not members of the EBEs, but are an independent group, also small in stature, who have been arriving here and want nothing more to come and go of their own free will, perhaps zapping our power lines for energy, but certainly not abducting scores of humans or causing the mutilation of cows and other animals.

First we will hear Ms. Tessman's first-hand report and then she will turn us over to Tibus, her space contact who speaks through her further about such matters.

The governments of the United States, the Union of Soviet Socialist Republics, and other Earth governments, have stored the saucers—or the remains of them—in top secret areas. Usually these storage hangers are on military bases, though in some cases, large corporations who contract with the military provide the hiding spots. This author recently talked with an ex-Air Force man who had top secret clearance during his military days. He gives the account of a chamber at Edwards Air Force Base, California, which is kept totally frozen by liquid nitrogen. With this area is an entire saucer suspended forever in cryogenic freeze! He also tells of a good buddy of his who disappeared the day after he breached security and walked into the building where this chamber is, out of curiosity. He never saw or heard from his friend again!!!

If alien space craft are kept under such tight security—and those who curiously wonder about them are "disposed of"—then what about the actual aliens whose bodies are taken by the military or "friendly" corporation with military ties? One can imagine the kind of security and paranoia which surrounds the areas where these ET bodies are being stored.

Leonard Stringfield's monographs on crashed saucers, The Roswell Incident by William Moore, and other reports on crashed saucers and their alien occupants, all mention cryogenic freeze as the method for storing the alien bodies (apparently military establishments are fond of freezing evidence of alien life as an "easy" and comprehensive "answer" to the dilemma of what to do with this "white elephant").

In several of the documented reports of crashed saucers and their occupants it seems that the aliens aboard the downed craft were not dead when their craft touched down on earth. In one report, one small fetus-like alien was moaning over the body of his companion who was being carried out of the craft on a stretcher. What became of this still-alive alien? And what of other aliens who were alive when taken into custody by earth governments?

At this point, we would like to give you information on this little known tragedy from The Free Federation of Planets (The Brothers) themselves. This transmission was transmitted to me by Tibus, who is an active contact with Earth in these latter days of the 20th Century:

Dear readers, this is Tibus. I come to you in love and light. I commend you for your abiding interest in our space craft (UFOs) and we who pilot them.

I am transmitting this urgent message at this time because it is vital that

117

receptive and kind humans know what has happened—and is still happening—when our saucers crash land on Earth.

Now, we understand that the skies above earth belong to Earth people. We do not interfere with military activities, we only observe. This is precisely why we do not use force to rescue our downed pilots and their craft. We have sworn our sacred oath that we will not interfere with Earth's natural path. We do have high technology which could wipe out all Earth militaries very quickly but of course we have never used these weapons, nor will we. We are beings of peace and love. Our weapons are defensive only, used to keep negative space forces away from Earth and other planets which are only now emerging into the space age. If you doubt my transmission on this fact, you have merely to realize that no UFO has ever used its awesome weapons on an earth government or section thereof.

And so, dear friends, when one of our craft does have mechanical problems or is shot down by the military, we do nothing to help it; we can't, per our sacred non-interference oath. The pilots and crew members of these downed craft know that we cannot help them. It is a risk they take just as Earth pilots take risks when on a mission.

If an Earth government decides to store away our downed craft in a top-secret place, this is acceptable to us. It seems "absurd" for the government to feel threatened by us that our craft must be dealt with in such super secret a manner, but this is Earth's prerogative and we respect it.

If an Earth government decides to freeze the bodies of our companions who have gone down with their craft, this is sad, but we accept it. We do not truly understand why our dead friends must be put on exhibition for a few top echelon military men and government leaders to inspect as the years go by, but, again, risk was accepted by our crew and personnel.

However, there are those of our Federation who have been frozen alive by earth governments. This is by far the greatest wrong and this is why I am now transmitting this information to you. We still will not interfere with the Earth government's decisions, but we do feel that we must let you know about this terrible tragedy.

Place yourself in the bodies of our Federation companions for a moment. You have survived the crash of your craft and you have been surrounded by primitive military men and weapons who take you off to an installation which is very secretive and prison-like. Earth governments realize that some of our crew members need a slightly different atmosphere than exists on Earth and they provide breathing apparatus for you if so requested. They attempt to question you, to communicate. They do not realize that you are a telepathic being who can read their minds' thoughts without verbal language being used. You know that they want to know the secrets of your people's advanced technology, especially its weapons.

You also realize that the people who are holding you prisoner do not have the wisdom or sense of decency not to misuse advanced technology which they now have!

You tell them nothing. You refuse to cooperate with them at all. You are threatened by them as they realize that you are not cooperative (plus, you know that even if you did cooperate, they would get rid of you after information had been secured). They torture you, usually with drugs or other "subtle" devices.

You still refuse to give information about yourself, the Federation, or it s technology.

They decide that you will be frozen alive, kept in cryogenic suspension until time itself stands still. You read in their minds long before the medical technicians arrive to prepare you for freezing (chemicals must be added to the blood to keep it from forming deadly bubbles.)

Dear reader, our Federation companions who have been frozen alive were frozen in a state of semi-consciousness, knowing the terror as the numbingly cold liquid nitrogen crept over them in a sudden horrible micro-second, freezing all parts of the body. And what becomes of the consciousness (the soul) of these companions of ours? They remain in a state of limbo, in a dream/astral state which is haunting and frightening...for they are not dead and so the soul does not pass on to other realms as it does in the case of actual death for all universal beings.

Often we, their crew mates, as well as Earth people, feel psychic communications from these poor souls, who exist as "ghosts" around the top secret installation where they lie frozen alive. Occasionally these Federation members have taken solid form, much as a tulpa does (a tulpa is a thought-form which the high monks in Tibet and we of Space Intelligence have been able to manifest as solid beings).

In other words, our frozen friends can sometimes be seen for brief moments (there is an old earth song entitled Have You Ever Seen a Dream Walking?) You see, Federation beings have a lot of force, a lot of energy in their beings; they are telepathic beings who are highly evolved. And so they are able to "manifest" in the astral state more easily than most humans could under similar circumstances.

We also wish to transmit that this terrible method of freezing aliens is used because Earth governments feel they might want to wake up the frozen sleepers at some future moment in an attempt to gain information considered vital. In a few cases, sleepers have been awakened and threatened that if they did not communicate, they would be frozen again. Each man and each woman who has been unfrozen in this way chose not to talk; we send them our respect and admiration for their bravery! They were then again frozen.

Cryogenics is a science which Earth is learning about quickly. There are private cryogenic societies who successfully freeze individuals who die but who want to take their chance that they can be revived in 50 or 100 years after a cure for their illness is found (needless to say, the freezings must take place 30 minutes after death has occurred). These people feel they have nothing to lose since they have died anyway. They hope beyond hope that they can be revived and cured. This is perfectly all right and we admire their pioneering spirit and hope. However, to misuse this technology and freeze any person or being against his or her will is indeed a sin against God and the Universe!

The process of waking a sleeper (unfreezing) is a complicated one which involves a total transfusion of life-fluids. Many of our frozen companions have "alien" life-fluids but their blood was taken from them before freezing, and will be used to transfuse back into them (as they cannot accept human blood successfully) if they are awakened.

The thing which concerns us most is the state of limbo these companions exist in, drifting in and out of reality much like a vivid "bad dream" which you may have had at some time in your life. These dear friends live a constant dream state, sometimes lucid, sometimes in the black hole of limbo and disembodiment.

At this time, there is nothing you as an individual can do for these Federation beings, just as there is nothing which we can do from "on high." However, we wish you at this time to be aware of their plight. This is very important! The time will come when your knowledge of this tragic situation will be of help to the sleepers! Please know that I have transmitted to you at this time and store it in your conscious mind. This is urgent that you do so!

Meanwhile, the dreams of the sleepers continue.. ..

God bless you.

May the healing light of God and goodness surround you always,

Tibus of The Federation

Here the transmission ends. There is great urgency and emotion accompanying this transmission. We should all consider it seriously! After all, what has become of the pilots of the crashed UFOs ...those pilots whose craft landed intact, who were not dead but were taken prisoner? It is an earth-shaking question of enormous implications!

THE INVITATION TO MEET A "VISITOR" IN THE PENTAGON

There are those who would go out of their way to try and discredit Dr. Frank E. Stranges' claims that he met a space being named Val Thor in the Pentagon.

These critics point to the fact that he was once arrested and thrown in jail for supposedly conspiring to smuggle marijuana into this country from Mexico. These same critics fail to point out that Frank has been absolved of all charges and even possesses certificates of appreciation from various sheriffs departments across the state of California for his outstanding work. They also heap suspicion on him by inferring that the various degrees he holds were obtained from "mail order mills" and that he did not attend a legitimate divinity college. This despite the fact that Dr. Stranges has for several decades dedicated his life to God, heading up the International Evangelism Crusades, preaching to millions in this country and abroad.

In fact, it was while he was attending seminary school that he first heard about flying saucers. "I was constantly running into young men in the service, who claimed to have been followed by strange objects while on routine flying missions. Officially, these objects weren't supposed to exist—the government said so!—but off the record, I quickly discovered that many officials in 'high places' were secretly 'very concerned' about the identity of these UFOs."

Because of his "close connection" with those in the military who share his strong "Christian views," Frank—who today resides in Van Nuys, California—was invited to visit the Pentagon and talk to a person who apparently had stepped out of a flying saucer three years previously and proven to everyone's satisfaction that he was not from this planet.

Suspicions among so-called "serious Ufologists" have long been that Frank dreamed up the entire episode in order to draw attention to his ministry, and thus to increase donations. Of course, anyone who knows anything about the "born again" movement (and they should from all the air time these ministers have been given on television in the last few years), knows that the mere mention of UFOs and space beings in some circles evokes images of the Satan coming down on a "fireball" with his legions of demons to enslave souls, and not to assist humankind, as the space person who befriended Frank in the Pentagon claims he was here to do.

Actually, if anything, Frank's claims are a bit more easy to swallow these days, as John Lear and others come forward to maintain matter-of-factly that visitors from other planets have been arriving here under our very noses for some time, and that at least one of these groups—referred to as the "Nordics"—actually are altogether human in appearance and could easily walk amongst us without the least bit fear of detection.

Furthermore, Frank's sensational story is also documented under the Freedom of Information Act, which makes references to a "blue-eyed 'superman' who spoke excellent English and could breath freely in our atmosphere without any devices." And while the memo which is marked 'EXTRATERRESTRIALS AND...'" (several words have been blackened out) is addressed to a "Donald Cook Jr.," there is no indication as to what government or military position he might have held, or who even wrote the message.

But why not have Frank tell of his own experiences, in his own words? For later on, we will use him for a source of information as to what our last few Presidents have actually known about the arrival of extraterrestrials on our planet.

The Invitation

One cold morning in December, 1959, through strange and unusual circumstances, I was invited to speak with a man from another world. This took place during an evangelist crusade which I had the pleasure of conducting in our nation's capital, Washington, D.C. The invitation was given me by a person who, for obvious reasons, cannot be named in this writing. However, suffice it to say that person is with sound mind and a good position at the Pentagon.

I had heard rumors in various states that such a man existed and was secretly being "entertained" by a few officials in high places. Howbeit, through my ability to follow orders, I was successful in passing the security guards in order to gain admittance into the presence of a man from a nearby planet.

Since that time, I have pondered this event in my own mind, over and over again. I thought how privileged I was to have had this interview.

The great morning came. The proper arrangements had been made. I was in a car, on my way to meet and speak with a visitor from the other end of our telescope. A man who gave me a feeling of perhaps being among those who, before me, have carried on similar conversations with men from outer space. As the car drew closer I began to formulate questions in my mind that I would place directly to him. I was then ushered into the vast network of the world-famous Pentagon in Washington, D.C. I cannot possibly express just how I felt when I followed the outlined plan for me to pass directly through the security guards. The next thing I knew, I was standing in front of a closed door. My host instructed me to walk in and commence with my interview, then left me standing alone.

Being a minister, as well as a student of the Bible for many years, coupled with the fact that I had been a private investigator, I felt as though my senses were functioning properly and that I knew exactly what I was about to do. I have always been keenly aware of fakes and frauds, even in the ministry; of this, I am constantly on my guard.

As I opened the door, to my left were three desks equipped with typewriters and other general office equipment. At one desk, which was back-to-back with another desk, sat Army "brass," busily engaged in what appeared to be paper work. The other man, a sergeant, was typing away. None of these three men lifted so much as their eyes when I entered the room. It was as though I did not exist as far as they were concerned.

I then saw one lone man standing with his back to me, looking out a window. As I approached him he turned slowly and looked at me. IT WAS AS THOUGH HE LOOKED STRAIGHT THROUGH ME. With a warm smile, and outstretched hand, he slowly started toward. I felt strange all over. He then raised his hand toward me in a gesture of friendliness.

HIS APPEARANCE: As I gripped his hand, I was somewhat surprised to feel the soft texture of his hand..,like that of a baby. However, his grip was that of a man. A firm grip that silently testified to strength and power.

His eyes were brown and his hair wavy brown, also. His complexion was not out of the ordinary. It appeared to be tan.

He was to all appearance like an Earth man ...but HE HAD NO FINGERPRINTS. Now, as a former investigator I have studied some concerning the proper value and classification of fingerprints in crime detection, as well as other reasons of identification.

HIS VOICE: The very first words that fell from his lips were, "Hello, Frank." His voice was very strong and mellow. It was filled with character and purpose. I then looked around the room again to see whether the other men would say or do anything. They kept on about their business, as though I was not even there. This is very difficult to understand, but there must be an answer somewhere.

HIS CLOTHING: During our conversation, which lasted about one-half hour, I asked him many questions. I took notice that he was wearing the same type of clothing as I. When I asked if he possessed any clothing other than that which he was presently wearing, he stated that he had changed clothes in order to give the officials a chance to run exhaustive tests on the garment...which they did. He then walked over to the closet, which was directly behind the sergeant, opened it and produced a one-piece garment that glittered as he brought it toward the sunlight streaming through the window; just as a passing thought that flashed through my mind, it looked like liquid sunlight.

I asked him of the material from which it was made. He answered, "It is made of material not of this earth." I further questioned him as to the tests that the garment had undergone. In sum, he stated the following:

1. They gave it the fire test. Temperatures above that of the melting point of steel did not even warm the suit,

2. They gave it the acid test. The acid rolled off it like water from the back of a duck.

3. They also tried to pierce it with a diamond-point drill. As a result the drill overheated, and the diamond point snapped, when it came in contact with the garment. The general appearance of the suit was all one piece...even down to the boots. It contained no buttons, zippers or snaps. I asked him how it held together. He demonstrated by holding the front together, passing his hand as though to smooth it out, and I could not even locate the opening. It was held together by an invisible force.

HIS PURPOSE IN COMING: He stated that he came in order to help mankind. He spoke in positive terms ...always with a smile on his face. He said God was displeased with the fact that mankind is farther away from Him than ever before, but that there is still a good chance for mankind to find salvation if he looks for it in the right place. He also stated that he had been here for three (3) years and was due to depart on March 16,1960. Claiming that he would not use force to speak with men in authority in America, but would be happy to consult with them at their invitation, he further stated that thus far only a few men in Washington knew of his existence in the Pentagon and few leaders have availed themselves of his help and advice during the past three years. The time of his departure was getting near at hand as yet he felt there was still so much to do. But his purpose would not be fulfilled by force.

HE HAD NO FINGERPRINTS: After I questioned him on having no fingerprints, he replied to me in his this manner: "Fingerprints are a sign of fallen man. Fingerprints mark a man for life." He also said, "Frank, you ought to know, being a former investigator, that one of the first things the authorities look for at a crime scene is fingerprints."

HIS HOME PLANET: When I asked him where he was from, he replied, "I am from another planet."

I asked him how many visitors we had on Earth and he said, "There are presently seventy-seven of us walking among you in the United States. We are constantly coming and going."

LIFE ON OTHER PLANETS: I asked him if there is life on other planets. His reply was, "There is life on many other planets, of which people on Earth know nothing. There are many solar systems for which man has not even given God credit. There are many beings who have never transgressed the perfect laws of God. Man does not possess the right to condemn the whole of God's creation because he himself has broken the perfect laws of God through disobedience."

COULD THE UNITED STATES GOVERNMENT DETAIN HIM FROM LEAVING?

I asked him what he would do if the military placed him in prison or jail in an effort to prevent him from leaving on March 16, 1960. In answer to this question, he simply stated: "Frank, do you remember one day after Jesus arose from the dead, he had gone in search of several of his followers. They had closed themselves into a locked room and suddenly they saw Jesus standing in the very midst of them."

He then smiled and looked at me as if to imply, "Need I say more?"

ANOTHER MEETING???

I asked him how I could possibly get in contact with him again.

He said, "Frank, when the time is right, I will contact you."

He then smiled and I felt as though it would be useless to pursue that question any farther. In other words, that statement was final.

I have attempted to bring you a moment by moment description of this amazing account. As I turned to leave the room, he said simply, "Please keep your faith and leave the same way you came in."

As I left his presence, I still maintained a warmth in my heart. I began to wonder who would believe me if I ever repeated this strange encounter with a man from another planet. I first considered not repeating this strange a story. But the more I thought about it, and the more I prayed about it, the more I felt that it would bring a great blessing to those who would hear and read it. I also thought of the possibility of being involved with the Government, but I decided to brush away all suppositions and fears and tell the whole truth.

Therefore, reader, you have the whole story. Read it over carefully and see what hidden message you may find therein. May God bless and guide you into all TRUTHS.

WHAT THE PRESIDENT KNOWS

It probably comes as a shock for many to learn that, while in office Ronald Reagan had an "obsession" with UFOs and a possible alien takeover. And probably well he should have, because as was revealed during the latter part of his term in office, Reagan had encountered a UFO while flying in a private plane, when the pilot had to alter his course in order to avoid a possible head-on collision. There is also a story going around that Ronnie and Nancy had a close encounter on the highway one evening on the way to a Hollywood dinner party given by a show business friend. When they arrived at the celebrity's house, Reagan seemed very pale and deeply disturbed. He told friends that he had been followed by a UFO as he and his wife drove along the coast of California.

Perhaps their eerie personal experiences were on his mind when he told the press following a meeting with Gorbachev in Geneva, "How easy his task and mine might be in these meetings that he held if suddenly there was a threat to this world from some other species from another planet. We'd forget all the local differences that we have between our countries and put up a unified front."

Later, he expanded on these views when he added, "How quickly our differences worldwide would vanish if we were facing an alien threat from outside this world. And yet I ask is not an alien force already among us? What could be more alien to the universal aspirations of our people than war and the threat of war?"

Truly, it looks like Ronald Reagan knew the "score," being fully prompted on the state of interplanetary affairs by his advisors while in the White House. Supposedly, after a private screening of the movie ET in the oval office, he walked up to producer Stephen Spielberg and commented, "There are only a handful of people who know the whole truth about this!"

But what of previous Presidents? Is is true that every one of them since Truman has known about what is going on, but has been sworn to secrecy by the military and national security officials who actually run the show from behind closed doors in the Pentagon.

Timothy Green Beckley, editor of UFO Universe and a well-established author of many books on the alien question—including MI-12 and the Riddle of Hangar 18—has researched this matter extensively, picking up bits and pieces of scuttlebutt here and there as he seeks out sources in "high placed" circles. His report is by far the most complete on the subject of what every President of the United States has discovered after the period beginning around the end of World War Two.

Within recent times within the hushed halls of Congress, retired Admiral Hyman Rickover made a startling statement "We can go to church every Sunday and pray," noted the gutsy Navy man, "but the Lord has many demands made on Him from many other worlds, and in the eyes of the Lord we are not the most important thing in the universe."

Admiral Rickover made this pungent comment during the course of airing his views on nuclear proliferation, which he feels is getting dreadfully out of hand as more and more nations hop on the atomic bandwagon. Obviously, the hero of many a battle at sea let it be known that he felt certain that we are not the only "civilized" form of life in the cosmos. No doubt, this observation was based on the fact that he knows better, because in Vietnam where he was in charge of our sea to land efforts, UFOs were seen flying overhead as a matter of course.

Every president in office since the end of World War II has realized the significance of our aerial visitors who have streaked across our nation's skies like they have carte blanche to come and go as they so please. Recently, under the Freedom of Information Act, it was discovered that all the branches of the government from the CIA, to the FBI, to the State Department, have at one time or another been confronted by this intriguing puzzle that remains in the eyes of many completely unsolved. Frequent sightings have been made by highly technical equipment and by trained personnel directly over our top-secret missile silos and near our most classified military bases. It is furthermore an established historical fact that for several weeks in July and August of 1952, UFOs played a cat and mouse game over Washington, D.C., out-maneuvering our fastest military planes which were sent into the sky to chase the unknowns from their perch over the White House and Capitol Building.

JIMMY CARTER SEES A UFO

Before Jimmy Carter became president, he promised to unlock the secret files of the Pentagon and release all the information in the government's possession on UFOs. He went back on his word some time after being elected. Nobody knows the reasons for sure why he did a double-take, but as might be expected, theories abound concerning what has become known in certain circles as the "Cosmic Watergate." "I don't laugh at people anymore when they say they've seen UFOs, because I've seen one myself." President Jimmy Carter made that statement on September 14, 1973 while at a speaking engagement in Dublin, Georgia. Reporters immediately pressed him to elaborate, which he did. He said that when he was campaigning for governor in the small southern Georgia town of Leary, he was standing outside the hall where he was to make a speech to members of the local Lions Club and saw a blue disc-shaped object in the sky. Several members of the organization were with the president when the object appeared. Carter ran for a tape recorder so that his description of what he saw would be accurately recorded. He told the newsmen, "It was about 30 degrees above the horizon and looked about as large as the moon. It got smaller and changed to a reddish color and then got larger again." Newsmen asked him for an explanation. He said: "It was a very sober occasion. It was obviously there and obviously unidentified." Carter was quite emphatic about what he saw. His press secretary, Jody Powell, told reporters: "I remember Jimmy saying that he did in fact see a strange light, or object, at night in the sky which did not appear to be a star or a plane, or anything he could explain.

"If that's your definition of an unidentified flying object, then I suppose that's correct."

Powell added: "I don't think it's had any great impact on him one way or the other. I would venture to say that he probably has seen stranger and more unexplainable things than that during his time in government."

Indeed, this is a curious statement Jody Powell has made, for we do know that Jimmy must have thought the sighting important enough, as he took the time and trouble to fill out a detailed three-page sighting report form and turn it over to a private UFO group which investigated the account. Furthermore, exactly what did Powell have in mind when he said that Carter had "probably seen stranger and more unexplainable things" during his time in office? Could it be, that the president has personalty experienced something along the lines of a close encounter? Or perhaps he had even been taken to see the actual remains of a crashed UFO and its occupants which the government is said to be in possession of since the late 1940s?

We can openly speculate upon the various possibilities for hours, but it probably won't do us very much good for, as we have seen many times, Uncle Sam isn't about to come clean and let us have the inside scoop which would once and for all clear up the mystery of the UFOs, and show that we are on the verge of some startling cosmic changes which will affect each and every one of us alive today.

PRESIDENT EISENHOWER MEETS WITH ALIENS

This story would be hard to believe except for the fact that it has been confirmed by many unimpeachable sources. One of those sources, the Earl of Clancarty, who is a member of the British Parliament, stated that President Dwight D. Eisenhower met with beings from outer space in 1954, and world famous language expert Charles Berlitz, confirms the story.

The date was February 20, 1954. Eisenhower was vacationing at Palm Springs when he was summoned to Muroc Dry Lake by high military officials. Muroc is now known as Edwards Air Force Base, recently popularized as the landing field for the space shuttle.

The President had a press conference scheduled for that day but never showed up for it. There were rumors that he was ill. The official explanation was that he went to a dentist. Newsmen, however, were never able to learn which dentist treated him.

Actually, Eisenhower was driven to the California air base to meet with space aliens. According to Lord Clancarty, the incident was reported to him by a former top U.S. test pilot. Says the Earl: "The pilot was one of six people at Eisenhower's meeting with the beings. He had been called in as a technical advisor because of his reputation and abilities as a test pilot."

What Eisenhower and the Six Witnesses Saw

The test pilot told Lord Clancarty: "Five different alien craft landed at the base. Three were saucer-shaped and two were cigar-shaped...and as Eisenhower and his small group watched, the aliens disembarked and approached them. "They looked something like humans, but not exactly." The test pilot described the beings as having human-like features, but that by our standards they were misshapen. They were the same height and weight as the average man and were able to breathe air without the use of a helmet or mask. The test pilot reported that the aliens spoke English and wanted Eisenhower to start an education program for the people of the United States, and eventually the Earth. Eisenhower allegedly replied that he didn't think the world was ready for that. The president said that his concern was that a world-wide announcement that aliens had landed would likely cause panic.

The aliens agreed with that opinion, saying that they would continue to contact isolated individuals until the people of the earth got used to the idea of their presence.

The President Watches an Incredible Demonstration

According to the test pilot: "They demonstrated their space-craft for the president. They showed him their ability to make themselves invisible.

"This really caused the president a lot of discomfort because none of us could see them even though we knew they were still there. The aliens then boarded their ships and departed." The pilot told Lord Clancarty that he never told another soul about this unique meeting, and that now all the others involved in the encounter are dead.

Additional Verification

A recent report in the National Enquirer regarding the Eisenhower incident adds a quote from UFO researcher Gabriel Green, who testifies that he once held a conversation with a gunnery sergeant that had been stationed at Edwards during this period. The sergeant said he and his team were using live ammo and were ordered by a general to fire at the alien spacecraft. Their attack was futile, however, as none of the shells could penetrate the tough metal hull of the craft and eventually the men watched in amazement as the ships proceeded to land near one of the large hangars. Additional confirmation comes from Charles Berlitz, who reports in the book, The Roswell Incident, that a man named Gerald Light was still another witness to the astonishing encounter. Light wrote a letter dated April 16, 1954, to UFO writer Meade Layne, acting director of the Borderland Sciences Research Foundation. In this communication he stated that he saw the five UFOs land at the base. "I had the distinct feeling," he commented, "that the world as I knew it had come to an end. It has finally happened—we have seen and met aliens from another world!"

AN ASTRONAUT BECOMES INVOLVED IN A UFO LANDING

Though it was some years later, it is hard to believe that this second landing of a UFO at Edwards Air Force Base doesn't somehow confirm the episode involving President Eisenhower. In this later incident—which took place either in 1957 or '58—Gordon Cooper (a man with the "right stuff" who was to take a ride into space) saw photographic evidence of an actual UFO touching down upon the earth. In a taped interview with NBC newsman Lee Spiegel, Cooper disclosed that after lunch this particular day, several men under his direct command who had been assigned to photograph an area of the vast dry lake beds near Edwards, came racing into his office very excited about something they had witnessed. "While the crew was out there, they spotted a strange-looking craft above the lake bed, and they began taking films of it." Cooper says the object was very definitely "hovering above the ground. And then it slowly came down and sat on the lake bed for a few minutes." All during this time the motion picture cameras were filming away.

"There were varied estimates by the cameramen on what the actual size of the object was," Cooper confesses, "but they all agreed that it was at least the size of a vehicle that would carry normal-sized people in it."

Cooper, then a colonel in the Air Force, was not fortunate enough to be outdoors at the time of this incredible encounter, but he did see the films as soon as they were rushed through the development process.

"It was a typical circular-shaped UFO," he recollects. "Not too many people saw it, because it took off at quite a sharp angle and just climbed straight on out of sight."

In addition, Cooper says that he didn't take any kind of poll to determine who had seen the craft, "because there were always strange things flying around in the air over Edwards." This is a statement newsman Spiegel was able to able to verify through his own research efforts, having obtained closely guarded tapes of conversations between military pilots circling the base and their commanding officers in the flight tower, tracking the presence of unidentified objects.

"People just didn't ask a lot of questions about things they saw and couldn't understand, noted Cooper, who adds that it was a lot simpler to just look the other way, shrug one's shoulders, and chalk up what had been seen to "just another experimental aircraft that must have been developed at another area of the air base."

But what about the photographic proof-the motion picture footage that was taken? "I think it was definitely a UFO," Cooper states, and he makes no bones about it. "However, where it [the object] came from and who was in it is hard to determine, because it didn't stay around long enough to discuss the matter—there wasn't even time to send out a welcoming committee!"

After he had reviewed the film at least a dozen times, the footage was quickly forwarded to Washington. Cooper no doubt expected to get a reply in a few weeks time as to what his men had seen and photographed, but there was no word, and the movie vanished without a trace, never to surface again!

Eisenhower's Warning

The report by Cooper, which was confirmed to me in a direct phone call to the astronaut several years ago, adds considerable substance to the accounts which say that President Eisenhower experienced a close encounter of his very own. Though he might have wanted to tell the world about what he had seen, the President kept quiet, no doubt told by his advisors that such a disclosure might cause panic in the streets. Around this same period we know for a fact that both the military and the CIA were concerned that civilization might come to an abrupt halt—as we've come to know—should word leak out that an advanced race of beings were coming to earth and had offered to exchange data with us all.

Before his death, it might be that Eisenhower had realized the error of his ways and that he had taken bad advice, for he warned that the big threat to our freedom would not likely emerge from some outside source, but from the military-industrial complex which he saw as working in cahoots to enslave society. It is pretty obvious, that this unholy alliance has continued to cement itself and is responsible for the state of affairs we find ourselves in today.

STARTLING REVELATIONS FROM A MAN OF GOD

Dr. Frank E. Stranges has had a long career in the religious sciences. Born and raised in Brooklyn, New York, he entered seminary school at an early age eager to learn all he could about God and the kingdom of Heaven. Today, Dr. Stranges is president of the International Evangelism Crusades as well as the International Theological Seminary. In addition, he holds many other honors and degrees, but most important of all perhaps is his firm commitment that UFOs play an important role in the ways of the Lord. While he was in college he discovered that many learned men such as military personnel, as well as pilots and police officers had been engaged by these whirling, twirling discs that have been seen overhead since the late 1940s. In December, 1959, an event took place which was to change Dr. Stranges' life forever. Through what he says were "a series of strange and unusual circumstances," he was invited to speak with a man from another world inside the Pentagon. The meeting took place during an evangelistic crusade which he was conducting in Washington. "The invitation was given to me by a person who, for obvious reasons, cannot be named in writing. However, suffice it to say that person is a born-again Christian with a sound mind and a good position at the Pentagon."

Dr. Stranges' meeting with Val Thor is a matter of record as written by Dr. Stranges in two books, and After the conference, Frank left the building feeling totally elated; so emotionally uplifted was he by his visit with a man of supreme intelligence whose only thoughts were for the betterment of humankind. Since that day, many years ago, Dr. Stranges has had further "eye-opening" meetings with this man who looks as human as any of us, but who has a love of the Creator and of life that cannot be readily found on ths planet. According to Stranges, Val Thor and other aliens are here—and have been here since Biblical times—to help with our spiritual progression.

Presidential Encounters

Recently, I had the opportunity to visit Dr. Stranges at his church, located at

AMERICA'S TOP SECRET TREATY WITH ALIEN LIFE FORMS

7970 Woodman Avenue, Van Nuys, California. The subject from the pulpit for the evening was UFOs and the Bible, and during the course of the discussion, I was invited to the rostrum to say a few words. Later, after a brief recess, Dr. Stranges decided to reveal some highly confidential information to his congregation. Through his relationship with Val Thor and the Space Brothers, Dr. Stranges and his high-level government contacts had decided to reveal a series of revolutionary disclosures pertaining to extraterrestrials and how they have influenced many of our presidents from George Washington down to the current Chief of State. Following is a transcript of Dr. Stranges' revelations:

· "George Washington had a spiritual experience at Valley Forge. According to the records, he experienced a space visitation regarding his own destiny as the first President of America. He never discussed it with his troops. He discussed it with his chaplain, with his wife and with close friends who also held high military ranks.

· "Abraham Lincoln, during the period from 1861 to 1865 was contacted by beings labeled by the press as 'space people', who accompanied Lincoln during his darkest days throughout the Civil war. He was warned by a space entity in a dream not to go to Ford's Theater, but he felt obligated to those who made plans, and it cost him his life.

· "Harry Truman, 33rd President, had his close encounter on July 4, 1945, just prior to August 5, 1945 when the first atomic bomb was dropped on Hiroshima, Japan. He visually witnessed more than 12 UFO sightings during his terms in office. According to two retired Secret Service agents, Truman met with space people on more than one occasion but did not think it expedient to relate his conversation because he did not want to rub anyone in the National Security Council.

· "In 1953 Dwight Eisenhower was the 34th President of the United States. In 1954 he was flown to Palm Springs where he left his wife. His press secretary told the world he was on a golfing vacation. Instead, he was flown by helicopter to Edwards Air force Base. Three UFOs had landed there. The pilot of the first UFO got into the second UFO and UFOs two and three lifted off, leaving the one UFO on the runway.

Military individuals dragged the UFO into a hangar and placed heavy curtains of security over the whole place. It has been one of the closest guarded secrets in history. The president was brought in, along with with several members of the Joints Chiefs, several members of the National Security Council and a representative from Rockefeller's office and a representative of the Rothchilds. Why were these key people invited to see a UFO that had landed at Edwards?

"When Eisenhower viewed the UFO, two individuals were able to tip it upside down. The Craft was about 30 feet in diameter. Everyone stood back and the strangest phenomenon occurred. The UFO dematerialized before their eyes. It has been claimed that they have motion pictures of this event. Then it materialized again. They say it was the direct cause of Eisenhower's first heart attack.

"To this day, the UFO has remained at Edwards. It is still there. They have brought in scientists from all over the world to try to figure out how to crack into that UFO. They gave it every test that they gave Val Thor's garment, including the acid test and the laser. The laser was put on that ship and it didn't even warm up the surface. It's defying the best scientific minds in the world. To this day, they are still playing with it.

"Mr. Eisenhower had to clue Mr. Nixon in on this. All he could say was, 'My God, my God, my God!' At first Mr, Nixon had doubts. It was disclosed that his reason for doubting was that he had not seen it himself. But Richard Nixon also flew to that place and saw it for himself. Every president since Eisenhower has been to that site and seen that ship.

"Other countries have pleaded to be allowed to take it to their country for tests, including West Germany. But so far no good.

GREAT SOCIAL CHANGE AVOIDED

"John F. Kennedy, the 35th president, had met many opportunities to help change the course of the United States. During the last three months of his life, in 1963, he produced a list of changes that he was about to introduce to the Congress. The list was shared with Lyndon Johnson, Bobby Kennedy, and the man whose name sprung up 22 times in the recently released CIA records, Henry Kissinger. From that day to this the list has disappeared, just as mysteriously as Mr. Kennedy's brain disappeared. When they performed the autopsy, they couldn't find his brain. The intelligence report says that his brain is in the Soviet Union.

"Jimmy Carter was very fearful of intelligence forces in Washington, D.C. He was also fearful of certain foreign powers, who had a powerful influence in the American government. Following news reports about his UFO sighting, the White House was deluged with letters and phone calls from so many people that he absolutely refused to discuss his UFO sighting any further.

'Every president, for the past 10 presidents, has promised that as soon as they become president, all UFO information would be freely given to the public."

RONALD REAGAN-MYSTERY MAN

"Ronald Reagan is a puzzle. He holds membership card number one to our organization, The National Investigation Committee on UFOs. He has had opportunities to meet with people from other worlds, who are far more advanced than we are. Because of his idea, similar to Nixon's, 'I must do it myself or if I depart from the normal way of doing things, I may incur the wrath of some of my biggest supporters,' he did not keep his promise.

"When he was running for governor of the state of California, Mr. Reagan promised that if he became governor he would start a state investigations office. This was during the last five days of the filming of my documentary Phenomenon 777. He was making commercials for the Borax company at the time. Fifteen days after he became governor, I wrote to him and he didn't know me from Adam's housecat. He didn't want to know me either, when it came to UFOs. He said, 'There are certain things that we can't get into right now. Wait until next year.'

"Next year became four years later and there was nothing. Then he became president of the United States and still there was nothing. He agreed to do something, then he disagreed. At one time he wanted to start the most powerful non-governmental UFO investigative body in the United States. Seven years later, nothing.

"President Reagan's life was spared recently by a certain Secret Service man who, to this day, cannot be located. During the attempted assassination, one Secret Service agent was so excited that he aimed his gun right at the president. Another Secret Service agent grabbed his wrist and pushed it up. That Secret Service man is gone. They have no Secret Service man that fits the description that was on the scene at that time.

"Not long before that, Mr. Ford was in a certain city in the state of California and someone aimed a gun at him. An invisible hand clamped down on that gun and caused it to misfire. I don't believe in accidents. I believe that all things are under divine control and everything is under divine power.

"There is still hope that President Reagan will condescend to meet with Val Thor or anyone else to help this nation find a proper balance. We need to pray for the leaders of our nation. We need to encourage as many clear thinking people as possible to investigate, prove all things. We must determine in our hearts to separate fact from fiction and hold fast to that which is true. We are living in a generation when anything good for the human family could happen. "

ROBERT KENNEDY'S DEVOTION
TO THE CAUSE OF THE SPACE BROTHERS

Even though he never got to be president, Robert Kennedy had great leadership abilities. Some time before he was shot down in a Los Angeles hotel, Bobby expressed a definite belief in UFOs. In a personal letter to publisher Gray Barker, Kennedy noted that he was a card-carrying member of the Amalgamated Flying Saucers Clubs of America (directed by Gabriel Green, a Yucca Valley, California contactee) and indicated that he accepted the stories of those who said they had encountered aliens from other planets.

Kennedy wrote: "Like many other people in our country, I am interested in the UFO phenomenon. I watch with great interest all reports of Unidentified Flying Objects, and I hope some day we will know more about this intriguing subject. Dr. Harlow Shapely, the prominent astronomer, has stated that there is a probability that there is other life in the universe. I favor more research regarding this matter, and I hope that once and for all we can determine the true facts about flying saucers."

While it is certainly difficult to prove, there are those who theorize that Robert Kennedy might have been killed because he was too "New Age," and because he had expressed an intense interest, not only in UFOs, but in many matters that would bring about great social change on our planet. As a footnote, it should be brought out that Kennedy's assassin had ample knowledge of the negative aspects of psychic patterns, and later, while in jail, he stated that he did not remember shooting Kennedy—but that he might have been hypnotized by someone into committing such a foul deed.

It should be pointed out that Robert Kennedy was shot twice from the back, but that Sirhan was in front of Kennedy when he was shot.

Doesn't it always seem like those who wish to bring about important social change usually meet with an untimely death? Maybe Robert Kennedy rubbed someone the wrong way, and perhaps that someone was a member of a group that has long tried to halt America's spiritual growth and keep this country and the rest of the world in virtual enslavement.

Furthermore, on the subject of Robert Kennedy, we have Dr. Stranges' solemn word that Bobby met towards his final days with the Space Brother known as Val Thor. According to Stranges' testimony, Kennedy once showed up at his Van Nuys home shortly after the dinner hour insisting upon having Stranges set up a conference between him and Val Thor.

"I told Kennedy I could not do that, that Val met with only those he wished to meet with. But I did recommend that Kennedy go into the next room and type out any questions he might have of Val Thor and promised that I would personally deliver Kennedy's message to my alien friend. Later, Val stated that he had gotten together with Mr. Kennedy and that Robert had wanted to know what his chances were of becoming president. To this question Val replied, 'Mr. Kennedy, four years from now you would stand an excellent chance of winning. But, I beg you to remain far away from the political race this year.' " History tells us that Kennedy did not heed Val Thor's advice and ended up perishing at the hands of someone whose devotion was to the "dark side" of the "force."

Val Thor has many followers who believe he is actually a spaceman.

SUPPRESSION OF THE TRUTH

Messages received through telepathy from highly advanced space people who have been watching over the United States since the days of the Revolution have indicated that many of our founding fathers received inspiration from "higher sources," though it was always left to their free will to take the right course.

During one recent transmission received from extraterrestrial sources, the following was stated: "The foundation of your country was originally laid on our guidance. We find it disheartening that your government officials would so easily turn from the light that has been given so freely to them"

This transmission, broadcast via telepathy to a New York City businessman who has been experiencing such mental encounters for several years, included this information about the suppression of beneficial discoveries by those in power who would not care to see a change in the status quo.

"There are many on your planet now who have had at their disposal much knowledge. Yet, your governments and your scientists refuse to acknowledge their great discoveries. Many times, these individuals have come forward and tried to release their discoveries, that which they have locked onto, only to find that society is not willing to accept what they are willing to freely give out. Such an attitude in medicine, in the sciences, and in other fields, has prevented your earth from developing faster than it has."

Could it be that there are those that conspire to hold mankind back in the "dark ages?" It may well be that a New Age of light, beauty, and truth could exist around the next corner if mankind were permitted to develop along the path to spiritual perfection, without being thrown off course by those who find it to their advantage to hold us back.

There are those in "high places," in "positions of power" who make great financial gain every time a new nuclear power plant is constructed, who profit from every stream that is polluted, and get fatter every time either the U.S. or Russia announce that they are going to strengthen their defenses with more missiles and atomic warheads. These powerful men are not anxious to hear what the space people have to say regarding any new form of technology that might put them "out of business," or a plan that would satisfy all political factors and allow humankind to live in total peace forever. There is no money to be made off peace and tranquility, but fast fortunes to be reaped from turmoil and confusion in a world whose leaders have seemingly gone crazy.

As General Omar Bradley so eloquently stated before his death; "We have grasped the mystery of the atom and rejected the Sermon on the Mount (THE MOUNT OF OLIVES). The world has achieved brilliance without wisdom, power without conscience. Ours is a world of nuclear giants and ethical infants. We know more about killing than we do about living. This is our twentieth century's claim to distinction and progress.

JIMMY CARTER'S CLOSE ENCOUNTER

Before he became President, Georgia's Jimmy Carter had expressed sympathy for those who believed in UFOs. After delivering a political address outside of the Lion's Club in Atlanta, Carter, along with a number of his close aides, looked up into the sky and watched a mysterious object cruise about overhead. Despite attempts by skeptics like Philip Klass to try and explain the sighting away as the planet Venus, Carter realized that this was something pretty "strange" he was seeing; something that couldn't be explained away in such mundane terms.

It was like nothing he had observed before, and hopefully if elected, when he took office he would make sure that the Air Force "came clean" in regard to its UFO investigation, which he was pretty certain had not been the case, at least under the auspices of Project Blue Book, which so many citizens seemed to openly criticize.

Unfortunately, once behind his solid oak Presidential desk, Carter's tune seemed to change. He appointed NASA to look into the matter, which is, in itself, a kind of contradiction, because how would you expect NASA to know very much about what's been going on a few feet over our heads, when their primary function is to send rockets deep into the reaches of space?

Sure, our astronauts have had their share of encounters on the fringes of our atmosphere, and even while in the blackness of space, but for the most part NASA had been—of all the government agencies—fairly cooperative with Ufologists, even providing researchers like Timothy Green Beckley with color photographs and transcripts galore, though "professional skeptic" Capt. James Oberg continues to deny the significance of these evidential documents which are a matter of public record.

Unfortunately, most Ufologists today are of the "armchair" variety, more comfortable relaxing in their recliner at home than doing any actual field work. They are usually content to take the word of those fellow UFO "buffs" that support their presupposed theories and conclusions. Normally, if they read something in the MUFON Journal or the APRO Bulletin, they will take this to be the "last word" on a given case or subject. Why bother to check for yourself when somebody else supposedly has done the phone calling already?

It's this type of narrow thinking that causes most Ufologists to walk around in a daze most of the time, throwing out the baby with the bath water because of what is essentially their own misguided stubbornness.

When the story hit the tabloid press that Jimmy Carter's private helicopter had been followed by a UFO after taking off from Panama City, they were smug in their conviction that the entire episode was "just a hoax" created by some freelance "stringer" trying to pay the rent.

Naturally, since the original story appeared in such places as the Examiner, they weren't about to take it seriously. After all, when was the last time one of these sensationalistic supermarket "rags" told the truth about anything? Shouldn't such a "wild yarn" be relegated to the same category as the 90-year-old Granny giving birth to triplets, or the latest reports of Hitler having been seen sunbathing in Miami Beach?

Only one investigator that I know of "got on the horn" and called overseas to talk first hand to those who were personally involved. I'm sure if Timothy Green Beckley didn't have some publishing deadline to meet, he might have even hopped on a Pan Am flight and flown directly to Panama to investigate what was going on. But as it was, he was able to learn almost just as much from thousands of miles away, as if he had been in Panama.

Ms. Linda Arosemena revealed to Beckley that she hadn't seen anything unusual in the sky on Saturday, June 17, 1978, at 230 PM, the time of Jimmy Carter's departure, but later when she developed a roll of film of the event, she was shocked to see something mighty weird in the sky next to the helicopter Carter was riding in. For there, quite visible in one of the prints was a Saturn-shaped device—a definite flying saucer-type craft.

In case you missed it, the report in Beckley's UFO Review was pretty detailed. It begins with a quote from Ms. Arosemena.

"I was watching the President's helicopter take off on the way to International Airport. He was in the country to sign the Ratification with officials of Panama. It was an overcast day, but I was standing in what sunlight penetrated the clouds. I was taking photos of the reception party that had welcomed him at Fort Clayton where I am employed by the U.S. government as part of their Defense Mapping Agency Inter-American Geodetic Survey,

"I can't account for what turned up on the negative," Ms. Arosemena declared, "but I can tell you this—I've never seen anything like it during the 14-odd years I have been working as a professional photographer. "

Taken aback by what materialized on her finished print, Ms. Arosemena immediately telephoned the Panama offices of the Federal Aviation Administration and was put in touch with one Mr. Frank Grba, an FAA official who was totally stumped, but had to admit that radar hadn't picked up anything odd at the time. "They were curious, however, and did request that I send them prints. So far, they have not contacted me officially as to what they think the object might be,"

Ms. Arosemena also revealed that she sent a print to the President in Washington, "because I thought he would want to see what I photographed." The only response she had gotten to date is a printed "form letter" thanking her for her interest in the President's trip to Panama.

The photo was taken with a Nikon camera equipped with a motordrive, using Kodak Tri-X black and white film, at 1/250 sec., f16. The negative is exactly the same quality as the rest of the roll and the previous frame taken 10 seconds earlier shows no signs of anything peculiar. Neither the film nor the negative have apparently been tampered with and it is impossible to take a double exposure with this type of camera.

"I'm not certain what I caught," Ms. Arosemena stated, "but the image is very clear and there have been quite a few UFO sightings in Panama lately!"

According to a front page story in Panama's Star Herald newspaper, the day before, on June 16, at approximately 2:30 PM, Brenda Reilly was fishing with some friends on the causeway at Fort Amador.

Suddenly her friend Sandra Chandler looked up and asked what the lights in the sky were. They talked about the lights being a plane or helicopter, but realized that they were neither, when they saw its shape. Before their other friends could come up the embankment to see it, the object vanished.

"It was spinning, moved forward and then it just disappeared," Brenda said, adding, "it was just about to rain and the sky was overcast."

Brenda drew a picture of it for her mother, Mrs. Velma Reilly. "It had a black inner oval, with a dull grey metal-like outer oval," said the woman. "It looked very much like Linda Arosemena's photograph, except that my daughter made the sketch before this photo was ever taken. "

UFO activity is on the increase in Panama, though very seldom do the papers carry any information, most reports being passed on by word of mouth.

One report making the rounds is that along the coast on one New Year's eve, both Americans as well as Panamanians observed a brilliant orange globe which bedazzled and stunned the many eyewitnesses. On another occasion, an employee at the Panama Canal Locks working the late shift was shocked into speechlessness by a glowing sphere that appeared out of nowhere.

"Unfortunately," notes Linda Arosemena, "there is no official agency to report these sightings to." The issue of the Star Herald that carried her photo did ask readers of the paper who might have seen anything "unusual" to step forward and issue a report.

It should be said that publisher Beckley has a reputation for being somewhat sensational in the way he's been known to approach a story. From our corre-spondences, I realize that his "tabloid mentality " of using flashy, eye-catching, "hyped-up" headlines has something to do with the fact that he cut his teeth as a free-lancer writing for the Enquirer, the Star and some of the other lesser grade weeklies that no longer even exist at the checkout counter. So naturally, we can't blame him for sniffing out a "hot story," but what Beckley didn't realize at the time was that this story was a lot more "solid" than he might have been led to suspect.

For what Beckley didn't know, is that Ms. Arosemena's single photo was not the only pictorial evidence of what would seem to be a truly "historic event." For while Linda Arosemena managed to capture the UFO on film without realizing there was anything "unusual" in the sky, a video cameraman recording the President's departure from a different angle managed to shoot the same scene on tape that would act as additional confirmation of what, in the end, would turn out to be a fabulous scoop.

As strange as it might seem, there is a full-length manuscript making the rounds, written by a U.S. citizen who teaches school in Panama. The manuscript is titled, At the Highest Level, and the book gives names and offers substantial evi-dence that the aircraft Carter was flying in was not the only vehicle in the sky at the time, and that Carter's life might have been in grave danger if the "bogie" had decided to "knock down" the helicopter.

To date, as far as I know, no publisher has seen fit to "pick up" on this script, even though it is very well written and very well researched. Is this "rejection" part of the overall conspiracy? Has the entire publishing industry been "bought off" so that you never hear anything more about this event? And if you do recall the original report, you'll continue to think it was just another "silly story" that someone "made up" to keep you entertained in the commode.

From my own knowledge, I can tell you that President Carter was "debriefed"about this incident as soon as he was safely tucked away on board the super fortified Presidential plane, winging his way back to the states.

It was at Camp David shortly thereafter that the top military brass told Carter about the existence of MJ-12 and Project Aquarius, whose stated purpose was "to collect all scientific, technological, medical and intelligence information from UFO sightings and contacts with alien life forms." Documents that have been passed around state that this file (which consisted of 16 volumes of documents) contains information that "has been used to advance the United States' Space Program," and was meant to act as "an historic account of the United States Government's investigation of aerial phenomena, recovered alien aircraft and contacts with ex-traterrestrial life forms," to utilize direct quotes from the documents I have, my-self, had in my possession.

THE CASE OF RAYMOND MANCHESTER

Today Raymond Manchester sits in a prison cell, a broken and nearly defeated man. He is behind bars, he says, for some undisclosed reason which seems to tie in with a number of things he came across while he was in the service.

One of these discoveries involves the AIDS virus, which he says was originally manufactured as part of a biological warfare program, while the second involves his witnessing the unearthly remains of two alien beings kept in cold storage.

If true, his account is a travesty of justice. The following special report was prepared by Sampsonetta Greice, Editor-in-Chief of BVI-Pacifica, and explores the case in greater detail, though playing down the ET angle for obvious reasons. It is a bewildering story indeed, but one that has great merit in our own exposé of the Grand Deception.

On September 13, 1989, the Editor-in-Chief of BVI-Pacifica was privileged to grant an in-person interview to Raymond Manchester, then and currently incarcerated in Great Meadows Correctional Facility at Comstock, New York. Mr. Manchester had written to us a few weeks earlier to request such an interview and to make arrangements for us to visit him there. He went to that trouble and expense because his mail is systematically opened and censored and it was therefore not possible for him to communicate to anyone what he wanted to say in a letter alone. A face-to-face interview was the only way in which he could say what he wanted without the risk of being censored. So once we had agreed to a visit to Comstock to interview him, he made the necessary arrangements, and we travelled there to see him.

He had good reason to go to all that trouble and expense just to enable us to make one visit to him. Below is given in detail the information he gave to us. He has been the victim of an enormous miscarriage of justic—one for which the reasons are not at all clear. We are therefore sharing this information with our readers, that justice may eventually be done and the mystery penetrated. Raymond

AMERICA'S TOP SECRET TREATY WITH ALIEN LIFE FORMS

Manchester's case is a flagrant and chilling example of what might happen to any of us when the powers that be find it convenient, for whatever reason, to rob us of our freedom and our power to act, whether or not we deserve it. We ask that anyone who had the information that Mr. Manchester needs, or a lead on it, please contact us at once so that we may send such information on to him; or that you write to him yourself, at the address given below, via certified or registered mail only for reasons which will become obvious, as quickly as possible.

Justice in Limbo

Interview with Raymond Manchester, September 13, 1989, at Great Meadows Correctional facility, Comstock, New York by Ms. Sampsonetta H. Greice, Editor-in-Chief, B VI-Pacifica

Address: Raymond Charles Manchester

86-A-201 1

Box 51 Comstock, NY 12821

Biographical Information: Born December 18, 1953. Height: 6'5. Normal weight is about 225 pounds (when he is in good health), almost entirely bone and muscle. He has red hair, now worn long, and is Caucasian, with very fair skin. (He may have been wearing a beard and/or mustache at the time of the incident described in the S I.A. below; unfortunately, I forgot to ask him if this was the case, so at this time it is not known whether or not he was clean-shaven then.) Currently Mr. Manchester walks with a cane, his limp being a result of neurological damage due to a gun-shot wound in the head which he sustained in 1978, apparently at the hands of a Ms. W.A., described below. He is a Vietnam vet (he apparently received no wounds during his hitch there). He has been married once and had a daughter by that marriage, now six years old, whom he has never seen.

Mr. Manchester is an occultist and a member of the fraternal order of the Knights of Baphomet. He would enjoy correspondence with anyone who shares his interest in this or related areas. If you are interested in the occult and/or are a member of a fraternal order such as that of the Knights of Baphomet, and wish to contact him, please write to him at the address given for him herein.

He suffers from bad health. He would very much appreciate any Magical efforts made in his behalf to help improve his health or to free him from prison, as well as the more usual, mundane ones.

Data concerning current imprisonment: Currently imprisoned in Great Meadows Correctional Facility at Comstock, New York. Sentenced to 45 years to life for alleged commission of homicide, conspiracy to commit homicide and related charges; the person he is supposed to have killed was James Hennessey (probably an alias), who was at the time living in Manhattan with Ms. W.A.

I. The Case at Hand

The reason for which Mr. Manchester originally contacted us, which he wanted us to communicate to the entire Marginals Publishing Network for him, is that he desperately needs to locate witnesses to the following events, or to make contact with anyone who knows where such witnesses might be:

A. Concerning matters related to the murder of James Hennessey, by a person or persons unknown. On February 24, 1984, on 77th Street in Manhattan, New York, between First and York Avenues, a woman threw a bag at Raymond Manchester, who was standing at that location at the time. The woman then ran off. The bag contained a gun and some drugs. The gun had been used to kill the aforementioned James Hennessey, probably by the woman who threw the bag to Mr. Manchester. This woman was Ms. W.A., with whom Mr. Hennessey had been living at the time, mentioned above.

This woman, Ms. A., has been married and divorced four times; "A" is her maiden name-Currently, she is about 45 years old, but she looks about 10 years younger, or at least she did so in 1984, when these events occurred. She now lives in Manhattan, NY. She is blonde. She has two tattoos: one is on her shoulder, and includes Mr. Manchester's name (he says he had nothing to do with her getting this tattoo, and that her choice of it was entirely her idea); the other is in her leg, and is of a snake climbing upward on her leg, its head in the vicinity of her genitals. She works at a hospital as a technician. She is highly emotionally unstable; uses hard drugs, including crack and cocaine, in addition to being an alcoholic; and is something of a sexual vampire. She is not herself an occultism but when she uses drugs, she claims that her experiences are taken over "by Satan," whom, he claims, then "uses her to cleanse society."

Mr. Manchester has known Ms. A. for at least 11 years, possibly longer. According to him, she wanted him to have sex with her at that time, but he has always refused to do so. He says that she set him up to take the blame for the murder of Mr. Hennessey, which he says she committed, and he conjectures that her motive for doing so was to avenge herself on him because he would not have sex with her. However, because of her history of alcoholism, drug abuse and emotional instability as well as other factors, her motives do not realty seem clear at all, and may be something entirely different than Mr. Manchester conjectures.

B. Concerning the death of Raymond Manchester 's mother

On or about the night of April 25, 1986 or the early morning of April 26, 1986, Raymond Manchester's mother died under extremely suspicious circumstances at her home in Queens, New York. She was found on or about April 26, 1986, having apparently died of a heart attack. However, in her arm was a single, fresh needle track from a syringe; she never used drugs. The inference is that a person or persons unknown injected something into her body that killed her, possibly a bubble of air which, moving along the blood-stream into the heart or brain, blocked a cardiac or cerebral blood vessel and thereby killed her due to heart attack or stroke. That hypothesis is strengthened by the fact that an empty, used syringe was found at the scene; whether or not it had her blood on it was not communicated to this interviewer.

Her name was Mrs. Marian Frances Manchester. She was born Marian Frances Butz, but later she used her stepfather's last name as her own, that name being something like "Gunnschennin," before her marriage. She was a Gardnerian witch, that is, a member of the Gardnerian school of the Wicca religion.

The night of or before Marian Manchester's death, the aforementioned W.A. was seen running from Mrs. Manchester's house and entering a Cadillac driven by a black man, an acquaintance of hers who probably had little or no idea of what may have been going on that night. At that time, Mrs. A. was wearing a white halter top and black leather pants. It is not known what, if anything, she had to do with Mrs. Manchester's death.

II. Irregularities In and Questions Concerning This Case

For reasons that are not at all clear, evidence in Mr. Manchester's case has been continuously and systematically suppressed by the State of New York. Both objective evidence and testimony against him in the matter of James Hennessey's death has been minimal. The main witness for the prosecution was the above mentioned W.A., whose testimony consisted essentially of endless repetitions of "I don't know" and "I plead the Fifth Amendment." The actions of the State of New York in this case have apparently entailed a number of outright illegalities. One of these illegalities, for example, one which would force his trial to be declared a mistrial and free him on default, is the alleged lack of the signatures of the jurors in that trial on the documents relevant to the trial, such as the indictment and those pertaining to his conviction documents which now are unaccountably "missing," and which have not turned up despite intensive efforts on the part of Mr. Manchester's attorneys and friends to secure them.

Nevertheless, Mr. Manchester and his lawyers have made no headway on any kind of appeal or on their many attempts to obtain material evidence or witnesses for the defense that might free him, His lawyer is apparently now in Jail in Texas on charges that may have been trumped up, while a friend of his (Mr. Manchester's) who has been helping him with his case is likewise in legal trouble for suspicious reasons in California. Mr. Manchester repeatedly warned me that people who have tried to testify in his behalf or help him in this matter have died under mysterious and suspicious circumstances.

Obviously if what Mr. Manchester says about the above matters is true, a great deal of effort, trouble and expense is being made to keep him behind bars; but why this is being done isn't evident. He himself thinks that the state of New York is doing this so that he will not be able to sue them for false arrest and wrongful imprisonment, by keeping him in a situation where his ability to make such a suit against them successfully will be greatly hampered. But it would have been far easier and safer for them to have just killed him and covered it up, if that was their motive.

Just as clearly, if what he claims is the case, then he has been railroaded. But again, why? Why not just kill him? Why bother with him in the first place? This interviewer's conjecture is that he is being kept on ice for some reason, for possible use in the future; or that he is being used as bait, to draw the attention of particular types of people. That is, however, mere conjecture and at this time is immaterial in this case.

III. Items of Interest

A. Item 1:

B. While Mr. Manchester was in the Army, he was a staff duty driver at Fort Myers, which is close to Fort Detrick, Maryland. As such, he had a Top Secret security clearance, because as a matter of routine he had to drive the brass into extremely sensitive areas of various installations.

One day, he was dispatched to pick up a friend of his, an M.P. who was at that time a guard at the Fort Detrick biological warfare laboratories. This friend had stolen from the labs at Fort Detrick a manuscript and two cassette tapes; he told Mr. Manchester that he had done so because he was royally ticked off at the Army. Be that as it may, he let Mr. Manchester read the manuscript and listen to the tapes. All three described in detail the technology by which the HIV virus—A.K.A. AIDS—had been designed, manufactured and stored at Fort Detrick, and the logistics and technology of the optimal ways of introducing it into various nations and populations, with scenarios of the probable results of doing so. The manuscript was by Robert Gallo; it and the tapes made it clear that Fort Detrick, under Gallo's supervision, had produced the virus well before that time and had stored it there for later use. It was also clear from these documents that plans had already been carefully drawn up for letting the virus loose on the world.

B. Item 2:

Because of his Top Secret clearance, while in the Army Mr. Manchester was sometimes able to check out things he wasn't really supposed to see.

At an Army Air Force base on Rice Island, New Jersey, a friend of his asked him if he wanted to see something "weird." He said yes, so his friend led him to a cold-locker, like the refrigerator section of a morgue, deep under the base. There in frozen storage were the carcasses of two small, humanoid but definitely non-human beings. His friend told him that the Air Force had found them in the remains of a wrecked UFO.

Mr. Manchester, who saw the bodies of these non-human beings first hand, is firmly convinced that they were of extraterrestrial origin, as his friend told him. But from his (Mr. Manchester's) description of them to me, they could have been anything from leprechauns to ETs, to creatures from an alternate universe. Further, from the evidence, as Jacques Vallee and others have pointed out, though the general public still thinks of UFOs as having their origin on other planets, wherever the things come from they do not seem to be extraterrestrial in origin (see Vallee's Dimensions: A Case-book of Alien Contact [Chicago: Contemporary Books Inc., 19881 for a comprehensive overview of this subject, including evidence that supports the hypothesis that in the majority of cases, the origin of UFOs is not extraterrestrial).

I believe him when he claims that the beings he saw were real. But since he saw them only in the context of storage in a morgue, with only hearsay from his friend concerning their origin and nature to go on, his belief that the things were of extraterrestrial origin is not the final word on the subject. I therefore suspend judgment on what they were and where they actually came from, though I do believe Mr. Manchester when he says he saw them first-hand, and what they looked like.

C-Inferences

It is barely within the realm of possibility that his present incarnation and other troubles he has endured have something to do with either or both of these experiences (cited in 1II.A. and III.B., supra), However, there is no evidence to support such a conclusion at this time, and for now, that will have to remain an untested hypothesis.

If you choose to contact Mr. Manchester directly, please be circumspect. Assume that his mail is opened and read by the prison authorities, and that it will not get to him if they feel that for some reason it says too much or the "wrong things." If you want to make sure that mail reaches him without being censored or destroyed in transit, send it certified or registered, and request a return receipt. This is the only way to be sure that it will reach him unmolested.

ABOVE A "TOP SECRET" CLASSIFICATION

So far, Operation Majestic 12 has been getting the lion's share of attention. Even the staid and conservative New York Times has published accounts of this super-secret military operation, formed in 1947 after the crash and retrieval at Roswell, New Mexico. The purpose of MJ-12 is to gather and analyze information —as well as deny its very existence—and to keep the lid securely sealed on the "Cosmic Watergate" at ALL costs.

There are, in addition, numerous other Top Secret projects that deal with the arrival of interplanetary visitors to our cosmic shores, So far, the military refuses to "come clean and acknowledge any of these highly classified projects. However, as the days roll by, more and more information is being leaked, as military personnel continue to come "out of the closet" and reveal the very existence of such super secret operations to us.

Here is a short summary of the various UFO-related military and governmental projects and their "code names" as verified by our sources:

PROJECT REDLIGHT—Established in 1972, Redlight's main function is to test fly alien craft and develop our own disc-shaped devices based upon the technology of the EBEs. As part of this operation, black, unmarked helicopters are assigned to act as "body guards" whenever tests are conducted. In at least one instance, known as the Cash/Landrurn Case, an alien craft driven by an Air Force pilot started spewing off dangerous radioactive rays and the civilians involved were seriously contaminated.

PROJECT AQUARIUS—A multi-volume reference commissioned by MJ-12, which summarizes the history of the EBEs on Earth, how they helped develop our civilization, created religions and control our destiny.

PROJECT SIGMA—Its purpose was to establish on-going contact with aliens which it successfully did in May, 1964, when a United States Air Force Intelligence Officer managed to exchange basic information with two aliens at a prearranged location in the New Mexican desert.

AMERICA'S TOP SECRET TREATY WITH ALIEN LIFE FORMS

PROJECT JOSHUA—Code name for an attempt to develop a type of weapon to combat the presence of the Grays using low frequency sound. This project came out of an early retrieval, when an alien craft was accidentally brought down near the Mexican border.

OPERATION EXCALIBUR—In an attempt to take back specific underground military bases from the Grays, a missile was developed which can bore its way underground and eliminate the enemy without causing any extensive damage to our facilities.

PROJECT PLATO—The name given to the illegally made agreement with the Grays, in which the government would condone the abduction of a specified number of humans in exchange for technological data.

PROJECT DELIVERANCE—U. S./Russian treaty agreement designed to "take back" territory seized by the Grays. The recent changes in Eastern Europe are a direct result of this project, as the

U.S.S.R. and U.S. realize they can no longer commit the vast number of forces there, should they have to be used at some future date as protection against the Grays' LUNA-Fortification on the back side of the Moon that is maintained by several groups of sinister aliens. NASA has known about the existence of such a base for a long time. One of the reasons for the aliens being there, is to use the Lunar surface for mining purposes. Photographs of their huge drilling machines have been published in various journals and books without a great deal of acknowledgment on the part of the news media or the scientific community.

PROJECT POUNCE—A team of crack military personnel whose job it is to rush to the scene of a UFO crash, neutralize witnesses, and sweep the area clean of all foreign substances.

GUIDING LIGHT—Operational program whose sole purpose is to convey false information and to spread discord among UFO organizations. Donald Menzel is said to have been the original director of this group, now headed by Philip Klass.

There are also in existence a variety of other programs which have yet to be confirmed totally at this time, and their authenticity is still being investigated as this is being compiled.

UNDERGROUND BASES

My sources have divulged a considerable amount of information on the topic of underground alien bases and laboratories, as well as other facilities currently being operated by the Grays. I am, however, planning to leave the majority of these findings for my next book, which will cover this subject extensively.

According to retired Navy intelligence officer Bill Cooper, alien bases exist primarily in the four corners area of Utah, Colorado, New Mexico and Arizona, though I certainly know of many more throughout North America, and the rest of the world. Cooper says that there are at least six bases, all of which are on Indian reservations in the states just mentioned. The bases near Dulce, New Mexico, and Groom Lake, Nevada, are the ones most frequently spoken about. The lower levels of the facility at Dulce has been taken over by the Grays, primarily for genetic experimentation. The huge underground facilities stretch for miles down long tunnels and are connected by a high-speed shuttle system.

Several years ago, an attempt was made to "take back" these facilities by elite military personnel, but the raid was unsuccessful and some 66 members of a squad of Blue Berets were terminated by the aliens in the battle.

There are at least seven different levels at Dulce, with Level Six known as "Nightmare Hall." This level is used for most of the experimentation by the Grays. One witness working in a slave camp under the spell of the Grays managed to break free of their insidious "mind control" and gave the following description of what he had seen:

"I witnessed multi-legged 'humans' that looked half human/ half octopus. Also Reptilians, and furry creatures that had hands like humans and cry like babies. It mimics human words. Aalso huge mixtures of Lizard-humans in cages. There were also compartments of winged creatures, giants upwards of seven feet tall and beings that were half human, half bird-like." One level below this can be found row after row of humans who have been abducted and never returned to the surface. They are being held in suspended animation in cold storage units.

AMERICA'S TOP SECRET TREATY WITH ALIEN LIFE FORMS

Said the Dulce slave laborer: "I frequently encountered humans in cages, usually dazed or drugged, but sometimes they cried and begged for help. We were told they were hopelessly insane and involved in high-risk drug tests to cure insanity. We were told never to try to speak to them at all. At first we believed the story, but later found it was just an attempt to hide the truth."

One woman I have spoken with was abducted from the roof of a New York City apartment building and apparently held underground at the Dulce facility. She was first taken to a cabin in the desert which was being used as a camouflaged entrance to the alien base. She was eventually escorted to the laboratories to be used as a test subject, but at the last minute managed to escape thanks to the aid of one of the Nordic-type, tall aliens, who befriended her and showed her a secret way out, down an unguarded shaft.

Back in the desert, she was rescued by members of the Blue Berets, and eventually flown back to Manhattan. During a debriefing session with the military, she was warned to remain silent about her experiences. Anyone hearing such a bizarre tale would certainly think she had gone insane. It was inferred she could be committed to a mental institution at any time should she refuse to go along with the cover-up conspiracy, which she was told was being conducted "for the sake of the country, and the sake of the world!"

Another story comes from a private stationed on the surface at Dulce. He soon realized something mighty "odd" was going on around there, but it took a while for him to put his finger on it. Some of those who seemed to be ordinary servicemen apparently were not!

"One morning last September, I was working on a routine job when another of the young enlistees, a mechanic, came in with a small rush job he wanted welded at once. He had the print and proceeded to show me exactly what he wanted. We are both bending over the bench in front of the welder when I happened to look directly at his face. It seemed to suddenly become covered by a semi-transparent film or cloud. His features faded and in their place appeared the features of a 'thing' with bulging eyes, no hair and scales for skin. I stood and looked at it for about 20 seconds. Whatever it was stood and looked at me without moving. Then the strange face seemed to fade away, and at the same time recede into the original face of the young man underneath. The dissipation of the imposed face lasted or took about five seconds before it was completely gone and I was standing there weak, my mouth open and staring at the young man who had come in with the rush order. The young man did not seem to be conscious of the elapsed time when I had observed all this but went right on talking about the job as if nothing had happened.

"This is hard to take but I assure you it was still harder for me. No one can realize a jolt you could get from seeing anything like this until they have experienced it themselves. It was several days before I had myself convinced that maybe after all what I had seen was real and that I was not suffering from illusions and the beginning of insanity. Days passed before I saw this particular phenomena again. The next time was later at night at the guard house near the front gate, on the way to work. I had purchased some small items and on arriving I went around to the guard house with my slip to retrieve my package. There was only one guard on duty. I handed him the check and he began to look for the package, taking his time. I waited a minute, then happened to look directly at him again. His face began to change. Again the face of a strange creature was imposed. You could see through the imposed face for a few seconds and then it became the only one visible (solidified is the word) and again about 20 seconds duration. Again five seconds for dissipation and the guard started to move normally again, found my package and gravely handed it to me and I walked out without a word being said."

In another case, an old illustrator, John D., does very painstaking work, but during his being on active duty at Dulce, he began to act very queerly. He would write letters to the President informing him of a plot under way to undermine the government, and to sabotage the base. He began to draw pictures of American flags, beautifully executed. He drew strange designs of mechanical devices, began to visit the library and bring back books on physics and advanced electronics. He hardly knew how to spell the words.

He would patiently explain something of a very technical nature which he shouldn't have understood.

When asked what he was raving about and why he was causing trouble by writing the President, John D. would say that he had been "sensitized."

"Last year, when I was sick, the doctor on the base gave me sulfanilamide. There is a new fifth column in this country that is tied up with aliens. Selenium is being slipped into the sulfa drugs, and this selenium lodges in the bones and makes the body receptive to extremely short waves, those in the wave band of the brain. Similar to the waves that can be detected by the encephalograph. About 300,000 people in this country have been sensitized, and at least seven secret radio stations have been set up in this country, and they are broadcasting to these sensitized persons, instructing them in the best way to perform acts of sabotage against our planet."

Strange vats filled with eerie liquid is where aliens are being "grown." Dulce's "level seven" is said to be honeycombed with tunnels filled with a variety of genetic as well as breeding equipment.

THOSE WHO CHOSE TO TELL THE TRUTH

The risks are great.

The rewards almost totally nonexistent.

Yet despite the obvious outcome of their endeavors, the possibility that they are placing their very limbs and lives on the line do not deter them from going before the public and telling what they believe is the truth-and NOTHING but the truth, so help them God. These are the courageous, the bold, the patriotic of our search.

Robert Hastings

"This planet is on the threshold of acknowledging that extraterrestrial surveillance by beings far superior to us has been going on at least since World War II," says Robert Hastings, an expert in electron microscopy, after meticulously going through nearly ten thousand documents released under the Freedom of Information Act. Most important of all is Hasting's claim that he knows the exact location where the United States military has stored the remains of two humanoid aliens found in the wreckage of a crashed UFO.

"The government has assiduously suppressed information about innumerable UFO sightings and confrontations with beings from another world. I am convinced that the study of UFOs is one of the highest priorities in Washington."

Hastings added that at least two different sources have told him the exact same location as to where the little grey bodies of the creatures found near UFO crash sites have been stored, but, the astute researcher insists he "can not betray confidences and compromise my sources just to satisfy the curious."

Stan Deyo

Because of what he discovered while an unwilling "guinea pig" for the military, Stan Deyo had to flee the United States for a new home half way around the world. Running as far as he could, the bearded scientist ended up in Perth, Australia, where he surfaced to tell his incredible saga of a conspiracy so sinister that it doesn't seem possible that something like this could actually transpire in the birthplace of George Washington, Abe Lincoln or John F. Kennedy.

Deyo had enlisted in the United States Air Force and was sent for special training to the highly prestigious Air Force Academy located in Colorado Springs, Colorado.

"We were the elite from all over America, especially selected for a secret purpose we knew nothing about," he told People Magazine, an Australia weekly news magazine not to be confused with the celebrity profile magazine of the same name published in the States.

"They got control of our minds when we were asleep and fed us the most advanced physics for months on end. Then some of us began to realize something was happening to our minds and we rebelled.

"After two years, they failed the entire class—180 of us. We knew too much. I'm speaking out now because I believe the world should know what they are up to, as well as for my own protection."

The way Deyo explains it, the Sixties was a turbulent period even as far as the U.S. government was concerned. For some unexplained reason, Deyo found himself in the middle of an "intelligence war" between the Federal Bureau of Investigation and the Central Intelligence Agency, with the CIA bound and determined to keep the lid on a brand new form of technology directly related to UFOs.

The CIA in conjunction with "big business" has for a period of years been in collusion, says Deyo, on findings that center around the development of a type of saucer-shaped, anti-gravity machine that originated out of an alien technology. According to Deyo's scenario, the U.S. is worried that sooner or later they will run out of conventional fuel and the elite and powerful will need a revolutionary technology in order to survive. So they contacted General Electric, Sperry Rand and Bell Aircraft to spearhead a drive to develop this new technology, which can whirl a disc-like craft through space at thousands of miles a second using the minds of the craft's crew members to navigate the Earth-made UFOs. This is where Deyo's training was supposed to come in handy, because of his intelligence level, he was to be made one of the ship's pilots as soon as his mental capabilities had been "stretched" through hypnosis and an advanced form of "mind control."

One of the most astounding things Deyo said—and this was almost ten years ago—was that he felt one of the staunchest supporters of this radically new anti-gravity technology was none other than the late William P. Lear—John Lear's father!!!

At the time, Lear Sr. was quoted by the Associated Press as having said: "I can't help but feel flying saucers are real, because of numerous manifestations over long periods of time with many simultaneous observations by reliable observers." And this is the clincher: "There are now serious efforts in progress to prove the existence of anti-gravitational forces and to convert atomic energy directly to electricity.. ."

For those who hold suspicions that John Lear might–at least sometimes—be responsible for dealing from the "bottom of the deck"—providing as much in the way of "disinformation" as valid "information"—we can't help but theorize about the significance of the above quote attributed to his father, and the possibility that some of what John Lear is telling us is meant to steer our attention toward aliens, rather than look right under our very own noses at an Earthly technology that may be advanced beyond what we are currently taught is achievable through modern day science.

We wonder if perhaps there isn't to be found substantiation behind the rumor that Lear Aircraft Company (a firm that John's dad founded) is directly involved in some sort of research and development project involving anti-gravity and the manufacturing of UFOs made right here on Earth.

One possible scenario is that John Lear found out about this Top Secret project—perhaps while eavesdropping—and this is his way of "spilling the beans" without implicating his father or anyone else as the source.

Naturally, we can conjecture about John Lear and his father all night long, but one thing we can say for certain is that Stan Deyo is now living thousands of miles from his homeland because something really frightened him and sent him packing, and he had to travel to Australia to feel safe from hands that he felt certain were trying to "reach out" and do him both physical as well as mental harm.

Robert Lazar

Robert Lazar is a physicist who once worked at the Los Alamos National Labs. He graduated from MIT. Yet interestingly enough, his past seems to literally be disappearing all around him bit by bit as if someone—or some group of people–were trying to turn him into a "non entity." Indeed, according to investigators who have tried to check on his background, his birth records have even done a disappearing act, his phone is bugged, and an assassination attempt was made several days after he picked up the receiver in his living room and heard someone yell "DROP DEAD" into his ear. So far, Lazar hasn't had the opportunity to speak publicly about his experience for how many would actually believe him? His story has, however, been the focal point of a continuing probe by Robert Knapp, a TV newsman with CBS affiliate KLAS in Las Vegas. Because of his locale, Knapp has expressed a special interest in the bizarre activities surrounding Robert Lazar, due to the fact that the majority of them have transpired around a top secret military installation known as Groom Lake, located in the Nevada desert. As a reporter, Knapp has been approached by several individuals recently, who, though remaining anonymous, all pretty much tell the same story of having seen and heard things at Groom Lake that were out of the ordinary, and which they shouldn't have gotten involved with. These individuals appear to be truly frightened beyond words. They seem to be in fear of their lives, and it was only because of this utter fear that gripped his being that Lazar decided to go on record and "spill the beans," as it were. For at this point, Lazar feels he has nowhere else to turn to for help, that if he doesn't "open up" and "start talking," about what's happened to him, he's going to be "dead meat," because the "powers that be" have the ability to wipe him out at the drop of a dime. And while this strategy may mean nothing to those who seem about to "pull the trigger," Lazar feels that they may not carry out their threat on his life if they know the world is watching.

The area in which Lazar says this all took place has been designated complex "S-4" by the military. It is a small part of the Area 51 complex located on Groom Lake. NOBODY-and I repeat-NOBODY! gets in or out of this area without a tight security check by special MPs who are trained just for this job and move almost like robots. A lot of the work being performed at S-4 ties in with Project Redlight, the government's attempt to recreate the flight maneuverability of outer space craft. It is all hush, hush-way beyond Top Secret-and though there are nearly 2,000 government employees involved in research being conducted mainly in underground laboratories, most seem fearful to talk about what goes on there in even the most casual terms.

Lazar says that he was hired because of his technical background, but that what he stumbled upon shook him to the very core of his being. He came across papers dealing with UFOs, and there were even some photos of aliens. And that by snooping around some more he discovered that there are actually nine different types of alien craft being housed on the base. The government is trying to tap into the technology of these alien craft so that they can make and fly their own disc-shaped device, which they hope will be far more advanced than any Earthly-made military aircraft currently in production.

Nowadays, Lazar won't come to the phone, but that hasn't stopped newsman George Knapp from giving a full account of what he has been told by this "reluctant" witness.

"Lazar says the discs at Groom are powered by an anti-matter reactor which produces its own gravitational field—technology that does not exist on this planet—and the interesting thing is that he thought for a while that perhaps it was just an advanced secret scientific project that our government is pursuing, until he looked inside one of the discs and noticed the small furniture. All the chairs were built for children."

Knapp's shocking comments were made live over the Sun Radio Network on the "Chuck Harder Show," a program that airs in 30 states. The newsman believes that Lazar was being "strung along;" in essence the government was providing him with a piece of the puzzle a bit at a time. "He would see a saucer one day, the next day he would see the hangar doors open and see all nine.

After that he got to see the inside of the thing. He also got to see a demonstration of it. He was told to stand back and watch this...and the thing lights up real bright ...I guess the power that's produced is incredible. You need to produce your own gravitational field and it raised up. He wasn't sure who was flying it, or was it remotely controlled, or what? He watched it raise up, did a couple of maneuvers and sat back down."

Though he is reluctant to talk about the aliens he saw, Lazar did indicate that they were the classic big-headed, almond-eyed, gray-skinned EBE types.

The power behind the extraterrestrial devices the government is trying to duplicate is something called Element 115, and Lazar is concernedd that they may let the hazardous substance get out of their control.

TV newsman George Knapp isn't about to take anyone's word on such a bizarre story. As a veteran journalist, he's been trained to sniff out the fakes and the phonies. However, as hard as he tries, he doesn't seem to be able to prove the Lazar is involved—for what-ever reason—in a hoax. If anything, the evidence points very strongly to the fact that his source is telling the truth.

After being at the S-4 complex for several months, he started to bring people out into the desert on certain nights to see the test flights which he knows are being made.

"He had the date of a couple of tests and on two consecutive weekends he took people up into the desert outside the boundaries of area S-4 and they videotaped what looks like a saucer coming over the mountains."

Knapp said on the "Chuck Harder Show": "Five different people that we interviewed that had gone up there confirmed the same story. We also had confirmation of other bits of his story from other people, a former security guard who worked up there, who said he had seen the saucers, a former technician also. We even found a Nellis Airman who had been on radar duty at Nellis Airbase which is just south of the area, and he reported numerous times seeing things."

According to this confirmation from the airman, the saucer-shaped devices would shoot over the Groom Mountains near the base at upwards of 7,000 miles per hour. Sometimes they would vanish in the blink of an eye; other times they would stop in mid air as if "on a dime. " In the publication, For the People, Knapp indicated that other witnesses have been found and that the story is far from being over.

Chester Grusinski

Detroit's Chester Grusinski cannot understand why the Navy or for that matter anyone else in the government refuses to acknowledge an episode that took place while he was in the Navy stationed aboard the carrier U.S.S. Franklin D. Roosevelt. The incident involved the sighting of a huge cigar-shaped object that hovered 100 feet above the carrier and which was seen by a good percentage of the personnel on deck at the time. Furthermore, the sighting included the observation of several beings inside the craft, which Grusinski is convinced were not pilots from this world. The episode in question took place in late 1958 between Florida and Cuba. A check of Navy records as well as repeated requests under the Freedom of Information Act have proved to be of no avail, as no records have ever been forthcoming on this incident. In correspondence with Ralph DeGray of the Private UFO Investigators, Grusinski gave the following full account of his encounter while in the military, and includes statements regarding the harassment he subsequently received upon trying to tell others what had occurred that day several decades ago:

It was between 8 and 10 P.M. in late 1958. It was a warm day with temperatures in the 70s and 80s. The U.S.S. Franklin D. Roosevelt, which was on a shakedown cruise between Florida and Cuba, suddenly seemed to be in a commotion. Grusinski, who was below deck at the time, saw some people running up to the flight deck, so he decided to go up to see what was going on. After a few minutes, the officer of the bridge was called to come up on the double.

When Grusinski reached the flight deck, he saw at least 25 people watching a strange light in the sky, hovering over the ship at some distance. After a short time, the light descended to within 100 feet or so of the ship. However, now the light became a cigar-shaped object with a row of square lighted windows on it. Grusinski stated that the object was about the size of a juice can held at arm's length with rounded ends. Below the strange object, what looked like "heat waves" were emanating from its underside. Then without warning, two "figures" appeared in front of two of the dimly-lit windows at the right end of the object, their dark outlines standing out against the apparent soft light within.

One of the figures had its arm up by its head, apparently to see better, while the other appeared to be walking away from the window. When the latter had disappeared from sight, the other figure also walked away from the window and disappeared.

After the startled crew had watched this strange craft for approximately two to five minutes, it began to turn red from the bottom up. Then suddenly, the red changed to orange and the object shot up into the sky and out of sight at incredible speed!

After the incident, a lot of Navy brass came aboard the ship, along with the Chief of Naval Operations himself! According to Grusinski, Air Force brass and Marine Corps brass also came aboard the carrier, as well as Captains from other aircraft carriers. However, Grusinski said that he did not know any of them.

Grusinski stated that the sky was clear and that he and the others got a good look at the strange object. He said he did not hear any sound coming from it, but a person who was standing next to him said he heard a "whirring or low pitch grinding noise."

Grusinski said that the occupants of the "craft" appeared strange looking (their outline), possibly due to something they were wearing. From their (the occupants) outline they did not look human, according to Grusinski.

Grusinski stated that some time after the sighting he found that he "could not stay in line on ship and went AWOL. After returning and serving brig time, he was assigned new duty stations.

About one and a half years after the sighting, from 8/8/60 to 11/22/60, Grusinski was in Portsmouth Naval Hospital having tendon surgery done on his left hand. While there, a Navy psychiatrist began asking him questions about the Roosevelt ship and wanted to know if he had seen anything "unusual "or anything that he couldn't comprehend at the time." Grusinski stated that he did not mention the UFO sighting because the psychiatrist might have thought that he was hallucinating at the time.

Whether or not Grusinski's going AWOL had anything to do with the UFO encounter is at this time pure speculation. However, there have been other cases where UFO witnesses have experienced strange psychological changes which appear to have been a direct result of the sighting or encounter. It would be interesting to find out if any of the other 25 witnesses experienced similar psychological changes. PUFOI and others are trying to locate other witnesses as well as people who have knowledge of the incident. Mr. Grusinski has provided some names and addresses of people who he says have knowledge of the case and these leads are being checked out.

Suggested And Helpful Resources

Podcast
KCORradio.com - Exploring the Bizarre
with hosts Tim Beckley and Tim R Swartz.
Broadcast live Thursday's at 10 PM Eastern/ 7 PM Pacific

YouTube Channel - Mr UFOs Secret Files
100+ interviews and shows archived.

Website
http://www.Conspiracy Journal. Com

E Mail
mrufo8@hotmail.com

Authors Pages Amazon
Amazon.com/Timothy Green Beckley
Amazon.com/Sean Casteel

Search On Amazon.com For Complete Listing Of Titles Under
Inner Light - Global Communications

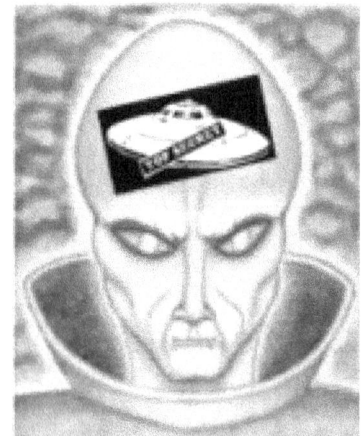

MORE NEW TITLES—MARIA'S INCREDIBLE "YES YOU CAN" SERIES
Supernatural Words Of Power

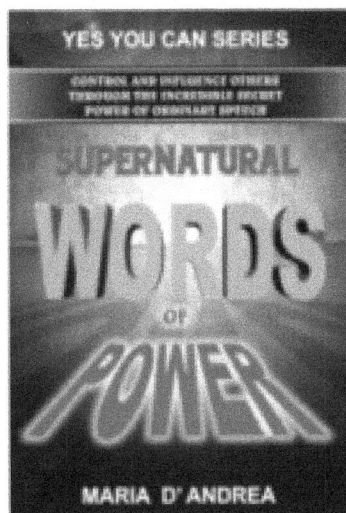

❏ SUPERNATURAL WORDS OF POWER
NOW IT IS POSSIBLE TO TAKE CONTROL OF YOUR LIFE BY HARNESSING THE SUPERNATURAL POWERS CONTAINED IN EACH INDIVIDUAL SPOKEN WORD – ORDINARY WORDS THAT YOU USE ON A REGULAR BASIS

We live in an age of high-tech communication. The Internet, cell phones, text messages and the satellites that power them are all a deeply ingrained part of our lives. But the simple art of speaking will ALWAYS be the most fundamental, meaningful method of communication as it is language that gives us the ultimate power over our individual circumstances and permits us to evoke love, good health and gratification. . . as well as fend off the evil and illness and despair that might plague us otherwise.

Maria D' Andrea is a gifted psychic who will teach you the hidden meaning of what you might think are just "ordinary" words. You will learn to harness the true power of linguistics, to use human language to establish an open channel of communication with the cosmos. This power was secretly embedded in an everlasting "code" by the Creator, an encrypted message which can assist an honest seeker in obtaining that which they deem worthy and essential.

In addition, this work will teach you how to "cancel" feelings of anger and resentment and even to neutralize the negative energies of your enemies.

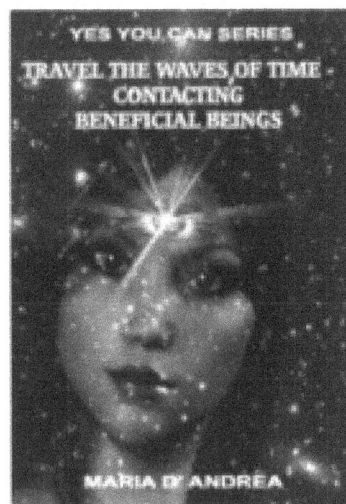

❏ TRAVEL THE WAVES OF TIME
YES YOU CAN! – LEARN TO TRAVEL THE WAVES OF TIME AND CONTACT BENEFICIAL BEINGS ALONG THE WAY!
Don't Be Frightened...They Won't Harm You!

According to Maria D' Andrea traveling through space and time is as easy as walking across the street, though you do have to watch for "unusual traffic" going both ways. In this workbook/study guide you will go beyond Albert Einstein and his "relativity" model of time as this theory is merely one aspect of the four dimensions of the space-time continuum. Science has its place, but the author of the "Yes You Can!" series teaches the reader how to skip the so-called "real world" preliminaries and journey – practically as an act of the will – throughout the past, present and future.

Learn to not only slip the "surly bonds" of Earth, but also how to set yourself free in time as you never before dreamed was possible. Maria can help achieve what may be the ultimate freedom a human can experience: the shedding of constraints of time. As an outcome you will be taught how to meet beneficial beings along the cosmic time stream, benevolent beings who can assist in guiding your life for your personal betterment – and without asking anything in return.

ALSO AVAILABLE IN THE 'YES YOU CAN!' SERIES

❏ **Evocation: Evoke the Power of Inter-dimensional Beings And Summon Spirits**—Spells in this book include: · Summon the Archangel Metetron to connect to the divine for information or healing. · Gain riches, honor and tranquility by the skillful use of various pentacles, all of which are fully illustrated. Use the pentacles to draw romance into your life or to safeguard and jumpstart that which is desired the most in any given area.

❏ **The Sexy Medium's Love and Lust Spells**—In this amazing book you will learn to: * Utilize the positive nature of Love Attraction Spells. * Develop Magnetic Power to attract members of the opposite – or same – sex!. * Maintain fidelity and excitement in love relationships! * Create love potions of the benevolent kind!

❏ **SPECIAL – EACH BOOK JUST $10.95, OR ALL FOUR TITLES FOR JUST $35.00 + $5 S/H FREE DVD OF A RECENT MARIA '"TRAINING PROGRAM" WHEN YOU ORDER THE SET.**
ORDER FROM: Timothy G. Beckley, Box 753, New Brunswick, NJ 08903

168

Over 150 Inner Light - Global Communications Titles Available On Kindle

Maria D'Andrea's Spiritual Life Counceling Mini Workshops And Seminars Now On DVD

Effortless And Immediate Metaphysical/Psychic Techniques That Work!

TWO DVD SETS NOW AVAILABLE

❏ SERIES NO. ONE

Disc # 1 - THE POWER OF PLANTING SPIRITUAL SEEDS - Create a positive transformation in your life through these tools of change.

Disc # 2 - YOU CAN LEARN TO LIVE A SHAMANIC LIFE — Tap into hidden knowledge to experience a new shift in consciousness.

Disc # 3 - DEVELOPING THE HEALER WITHIN — Here are principles allowing you to become self empowered.

❏ SERIES NO. TWO

Disc # 1 - ATTRACTING RELATIONSHIPS — Learn importance of applying ancient methods to enhance your opportunities with the use of colors, gemstones and astrological periods best for men and women.

Disc # 2 - SURRENDER YOURSELF TO A POSITIVE LIFE — Spirits will assist you in having a more fulfilling life. Learn to release yourself from the past.

Disc # 3 - ANGELS AND THE FALL — Work with Archangel Ariel and Zavael with specific techniques to help calm the storm in your life and create a more positive being.

ORDER INFORMATION - Each set of DVDs by Maria is $21.95. Or both for just $35.00. Add $5 S/H

NIKOLA TESLA'S "MIRACLE" ENERGY PLATES

3 SIZES NOW AVAILABLE!

Though not approved by the FDA or AMA, regular users say the plates function as Transceivers, creating a field of energy around themselves. This energy is very beneficial to ALL living things.

❏ **LARGE PLATE**- Approx 12x12. Best for using under mattress, chair or in refrigerator to keep food fresh. Ease muscle tension, anxiety. — $75 or 3 for $200 + $8 S/H

❏ **SMALL PLATE**. - Approx. 4x2. For litter box to keep fresh. Flowers live longer. Under car seat. — $25 each. 3 for $68 + $5 S/H

❏ **LARGE DISC** - Create necklace, earings for yourself. Use as animal collar. Carry in wallet or shoe. — $17.50 each. 3 for $40 + $5 S/H

SPECIAL - ONE OF EACH SIZE $112 +$8 S/H FREE *"HOW TO USE TESLA PLATES"* DVD WITH MARIA D' ANDREA AND PRINTED REPORT ON MANY BENEFITS.

Timothy Green Beckley
Box 753
New Brunswick, NJ 08903
MRUFO8@hotmail.com

Free DVD and report with all orders.

AND THE TRUTH SHALL SET YOU FREE!

Our books, products and services are for experimental purposes. They are not endorsed by the AMA, FDA or any other federal or local agency. We offer our merchandise on a non-returnable basis to those who seek the truth about matters neglected by the "Establishment." We appreciate your patronage and hope you will tell all your like-minded friends about our publications.
—Timothy G. Beckley

www.conspiracyjournal.com/
www.teslasecretlab.com

BUY TWO BOOKS FROM THIS PAGE— GET THE 3RD FREE!

WE CAN AWAKEN THE "DEAD!" Evidence Of An Afterlife Now

Vice Admiral W. Usborne Moore

In 1877, the author developed a profound interest in spiritualism, coming to an abrupt change in attitude, having by that time seen ample proof of life in a parallel world after the condition we call death.

Stated the author: "To be brief, I found that the deeper I went into the study of spiritism the more apparent it became that, whether he wished it or not, man's individuality was not extinguished at death. Through all I was constantly reminded of the existence of a near and dear relative, older than myself, who passed away thirty-seven years ago in the prime of her life. Her continued reappearances could only lead me to one conclusion: I was being guided to a reconsideration of the problem of immortality."

At a séance held on February 1, 1909, 19 spirits manifested, 10 of them for the author, including his father, mother, and his guide, Iola. "During this séance, I saw several spirits dematerialize," he recorded. "Some descended into the floor slowly and, so to speak, naturally. It was possible to follow their heads with the eye until the shoulders were level with the carpet."

This is among the most earth shaking books on the subject. It has been unavailable for many years. This is our private, collectors' edition.

❏ ORDER: WE CAN AWAKEN THE "DEAD!"—Approximately 400 large format pages, $24.00

❏ **THIRTY YEARS AMONG THE DEAD: Complete and Unabridged — Obsessions And "Curses" Removed Through The Work Of The Medium Mrs. Wickland**

Details the studies of of Dr. Carl A Wickland and his wife, medium Anna Wickland who cured many obsessed persons, persuading discarnate spirits to give up their hold on their victims, thus restoring their patients to normal, happy lives. Together, for more than a quarter of a century they "conversed" with spirits of the dead who had lead less than exemplary lives while inhabiting a human body. They had been the worse lowlifes – criminals, alcoholics, drug users, wife beaters, and the all around depraved..Many of Dr. Wickland's patients had given up all hope of a sane existence. Originally they relied upon conventional neurological methods of treatment which did not work. As opposed to trusting in the doctor and his spiritualist spouse who could communicate with those on the other side of the veil. Here is the eerie paranormal "truth" as Dr. Wickland saw it, about: Spirits and Crime. – Spirits and Suicide. - Spirits and Narcotics, Insobriety and Amnesia – Tormented Spirits. - Marriage Disturbances and much more. **400 large format pages. $24.00**

❏ **SPECIAL FREE OFFER** Order both works above for just **$39.95 + $8 S/H** and we will include a *FREE copy of DARK SEANCE* edited by Tim Beckley detailing the mediumistic abilities of the Davenport Brothers who are said to have been either the best mediums or the biggest frauds of all time. Their public séances could only be categorized as amazing. The brothers were bound hand and foot so they could not move. Once bound, they were placed inside a locked cabinet where their very theatrical demonstration would begin—first with disembodied voices, musical instruments sounding loudly and emerging from the upper portion of the cabinet, and causing quite a visual spectacle. They were chased out of towns. Their lives were in constant danger. One woman is said to have fallen to her death from a balcony.

❏ Order separately for just $18.00 or receive FREE when you accept our offer above.

Order From: TIMOTHY G. BECKLEY, BOX 753, NEW BRUNSWICK, NJ 08903

AMERICA'S TOP SECRET TREATY WITH ALIEN LIFE FORMS

❏ NAZI UFO TIME TRAVELERS

We are plummeting toward a world under fascist domination – a nightmare in which sadistic, jackbooted thugs are waiting for us to "catch up" in time with our own predestined subjugation to open worldwide rule by the Nazis possibly hiding out on the surface of the moon or at "secret cities" under the Poles? In the upper echelon of the military it is realized that "ETs" are not so much interplanetary as they are time travelers. States one Navy Commander: "They are extra-temporal. The visitors are clearly from the future. And there is reason to believe that they may even be 'us' from a future Earth." Die Glocke, or The Bell, may have been used to bend space and time and give the Nazis the unthinkable power to explore the past freely and even to determine our future. Here is evidence that a top secret brigade of Nazi engineers worked in conjunction with off world Aryan looking interstellar cosmonauts to establish space flight and time travel. These same Nazi war criminals were eventually bought to America under the auspicious of Project Paperclip to continue their programs.

❏ CRYPTID CREATURES FROM DARK DOMAINS: DOGMEN, DEVIL HOUNDS, PHANTOM CANINES AND REAL WEREWOLVES

Here is startling research from Pennsylvania' researcher Butch Witkowski, who finds himself in the middle of an unprecedented wave of "bipedal canine" encounters with hunters and campers. These Dogmen are upright creatures, standing over seven-feet-tall and said to have a muscular physique similar to Arnold Schwarzenegger. The strange hairy frame is topped by the face of a hideous, snarling dog who breathes out dread and fear to all those who cross its path. There are also dozens of reports of devilish, gruesome, repugnant, mysterious beasts - said to be Satan's watchdogs who protect the portals to other dimensions where no mortal dares tread! Here Is Proof That These Strange Canines Exist And Could Be Hiding In Plain Sight In Your Neighborhood! Read Case Histories Of Face-To-Face Confrontations With Anomalous "Monsters" And Incredible Beasts Who Spring Forth From The Backwoods, Other Realms And Far Flung Dimensions!

❏ SPOOKY TREASURE TROVE FIND OUT THE CONNECTION BETWEEN UFOS, GHOSTS, CURSES, PIECES OF EIGHT AND THE SUPERNATURAL

In this 398 page opus you'll learn of the "supernatural treasure hunting connection" that includes UFOs, ghosts, Native Americans spirits and even Bigfoot, whom are either guarding vast treasures or have been known to lead deserving souls to the end of a rainbow.

** For example, the late "UFO prophet" Ted Owens recounts a séance at a hotel in Durango, where he recovered a concealed treasure. ** Writer Sean Casteel reports on eerie happenings on a mountain in Oregon, where a slave's ghost guards over the treasure of pirates who killed him. ** And prolific Scott Corrales provides stories of supernatural guardians of treasure that stretch from South America to Lebanon. ** There is also Preston Dennett's experience with "spook lights," as well as Tim and Charla's encounter with the ghosts of Jerome, Arizona, and the famous Phoenix Lights and their possible tie with the Lost Dutchman Mine.** And let's not forget the Money Pit, subject of a History Channel series. Shiver me timbers! It's all here – and a heck of a lot more, matey. Could help you find a treasure of your very own!

ORDER FROM: Timothy G. Beckley, Box 753, New Brunswick, NJ 08903

172

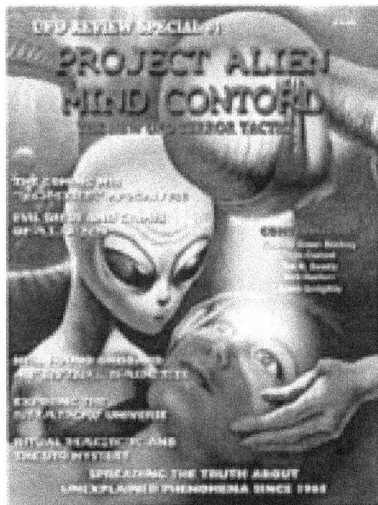

173

www.ingramcontent.com/pod-product-compliance
Lightning Source LLC
Chambersburg PA
CBHW081152270326
41930CB00014B/3122